Between Romanticism and Modernism

Four Studies in the Music of the Later Nineteenth Century

Carl Dahlhaus

Translated by Mary Whittall

Includes the Nietzsche fragment,
"On Music and Words,"
translated by Walter Kaufmann

University of California Press

BERKELEY · LOS ANGELES · LONDON

Originally published in German by Musikverlag Emil Katzbichler, Munich, 1974, in the series *Berliner Musikwissenschaftliche Arbeiten*, edited by Carl Dahlhaus and Rudolf Stephan, under the title *Zwischen Romantik und Moderne: Vier Studien zur Musikgeschichte des späteren 19. Jahrhunderts.*

"On Music and Words," by Friedrich Nietzsche, translated by Walter Kaufmann, was originally published in *Denver Quarterly*, vol. 13, no. 1, Spring 1978.

University of California Press
Berkeley and Los Angeles, California
University of California Press, Ltd.
London, England

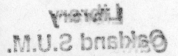

Contents

"Neo-romanticism"

❧

1

The present age has an apparently insatiable appetite for the music of the past, but that observation conveys nothing about the degree of musico-historical insight enjoyed by the listeners. Meanwhile, to the music historian who is not deceived by the appearance of familiarity and does not equate aesthetic habituation with historical understanding, the second half of the nineteenth century, the period from 1850 to 1890 that provides the staple diet in our concert halls and opera houses, is less accessible than the Trecento or Quattrocento, whose musico-historical outlines are well established. And the primary obstacle in his way is by no means an all too slight and fragmentary knowledge of such peripheral figures as Raff and Goldmark, Bruch and Gernsheim, but the uncertainty of historical judgments (not, let it be said, of aesthetic judgments) concerning central works by Wagner and Liszt, Brahms and Bruckner.

As yet hardly any attempt has been made to present the history of music in this period in a form other than that of monographs about the leading composers, interspersed with occasional outlines of cultural history which find room for the "minor masters." The history of music in the nine-

1

teenth century, unlike that of the fifteenth or sixteenth, is still seen primarily as the history of its heroes—the "great masters," the composers of the works which constitute the "canon"—but simply to condemn this one-sided emphasis as arbitrary does not take us much further.

For one thing, those who write history are not unaffected by the motives that stimulate the interest of a more general public in the subject under discussion. (A strictly autonomous historical method, one that was governed exclusively by considerations acknowledged only by other historians, would be as sterile as it was purist.) If music historians are apt to write the history of great men when faced with the nineteenth century, and to write cultural history when they tackle the Trecento, the reasons lie in the prehistory of academic historiography. Composers' biographies were being written before anyone embarked on the history of the nineteenth century, and the study of the art and culture of the Trecento as a source of "pictures from the past" preceded more systematic historical research. (Even today, the music of the Trecento is listened to primarily as a specimen of medieval culture, while books on the music history of the nineteenth century are read for the biographical keys they can supply to the "canonical" works.)

Secondly, the heart of the "aesthetic religion" of the nineteenth century was the cult of genius. And the spirit in which the musical facts were received and interpreted is itself a fact that shapes and motivates their history, and as such it must be taken into account by the historian. The principle that a past era must be surveyed in the light of its own preconceptions should not erect a barrier to understanding. It does not mean that one ought not to entertain ideas about the era that it did not, or could not, hold itself, but it does mean that the likelihood of arriving at pertinent insights is greater if one begins by mastering the categories of that era heuristically than if one ignores them from the first or merely dismisses them as ideologically untenable. Much would be lost by outright substitution of a structuralist interpretation for the biographical emphasis in the history of nineteenth-century music; it is enough to recognize that the latter is only one side of the story and to complement it with accounts based on other premises.

Thirdly, one of the fundamental tenets of popular aesthetic theory in the nineteenth century was that compositions were fragments of autobiography: such was the view of "poetic" works at least, "poetry" being the distinguishing characteristic of "art." The expressive theory of aesthetics provided the soil in which biography, often bearing a marked resemblance to the novel, flourished alongside historiography with a strong biographical tendency. It would be excessively rigorous to set aside the popular aesthetic conceptions of the nineteenth century as pitiable errors which the period entertained about itself, and to treat phenomena such as the cult of genius and the expressive theory of aesthetics, with its emphasis on (almost always idealized) biography, merely as subjects for dissociated analysis and scrutiny; they should be given their historical due as factors influencing attitudes and developments. The history of nineteenth-century music would lose a substantial part of its "local color" if it was confined to the history of its structures.

This plea for some recognition of the merits of the nineteenth-century biographical method should not, however, be mistaken for a demand for its restoration. The aesthetic foundations and implications of the biographical premise in music historiography are indeed questionable, but the disrepute into which, as a result, it has fallen in present-day theory is so exaggerated that a sense of justice drives one to proffer some sort of apology on its behalf. On the other hand it persists so obstinately in practice (if the practice of writing music history is in the hands of the publicists rather than the scholars, if the music historians cannot bring themselves actually to write music history, it is because they find the older methods obsolete and the up-to-date postulates barely realizable) that some emphasis on structuralist history must be made a priority if we are to avoid a situation where ever stricter formulations of methodological postulates will hinder or prevent their realization, and, conversely, delays in the introduction of changes in historiographical practice will provoke a hardening of theory into ever more abstract radicalism.

2

To German music historians of the traditional school—popular as well as academic—the second half of the nineteenth century is the age of Wagner or of "neo-romanticism." Yet Wagner's very pre-eminence makes it all the harder to relate the specifically musical mode of thought of which the *Ring, Tristan* and *Parsifal* are the expressions to the non-musical trends of the age; that is, to comprehend them historically—in their context—and not merely aesthetically, as isolated, self-sufficient structures. The difficulty is not simply a matter of the incommensurability of Wagner's work, but the size of the gulf separating music in general, not just Wagner's, from the important art and literature of the age. It is hard to reconcile this fact with the belief in the unity of the zeitgeist in every manifestation of an age, which is the fundamental thesis of the *"Geistesgeschichte"* school of the history of ideas.

It was this difficulty that prompted the historians of ideas to attach the label "neo-romantic" to music from 1850 onwards. The term originated, in the early nineteenth century, in literary theory, where it was used consistently to distinguish each successive kind of romanticism from the preceding one: at first the romanticism of circa 1800 from the literature of the Middle Ages and the early modern era; then French romanticism of 1830 onwards from the German romanticism of circa 1800; finally the revived romanticism of circa 1900 from the original, paradigmatic romanticism of a century earlier.[1]

1. R. Grimm, "Zur Wortgeschichte des Begriffs 'Neuromantik'," in *Das Nachleben der Romantik in der modernen deutschen Literatur*, ed. W. Paulsen (Heidelberg, 1969), pp. 32–50.

There is a certain wry irony in the classification of Wagner as a "neo-romantic" alongside Liszt and Berlioz, since he himself used the term polemically in *Opera and Drama* in 1851 for the French romanticism of 1830 onwards, naming Berlioz and Meyerbeer—a curious pairing—as its musical representatives. Such romanticism he regarded as a distortion of, and falling-off from, the real thing, and he made a sharp distinction between it and his own music drama.[2]

It was their own thesis that all the arts in any one period are permeated by the same zeitgeist that prevented the historians of ideas from recognizing the real element of truth in the label they applied to music after 1850 as a matter of expediency.[3] In spite of all the questions it begs, "neo-romantic" is appropriate if it is interpreted as acknowledging the fact that the music of the second half of the nineteenth century was still romantic, while the current of the age as expressed in literature and painting had moved on to realism and impressionism. E. T. A. Hoffmann's claim that music was the only truly romantic art can be disputed as a timeless, universal maxim (which is how he meant it), but as a forecast of developments in the nineteenth century it was remarkably accurate.

Early nineteenth-century music could be said to be romantic in an age of romanticism, which produced romantic poetry and painting and even romantic physics and chemistry, whereas the neo-romanticism of the later part of the century was romantic in an unromantic age, dominated by positivism and realism. Music, *the* romantic art, had become "untimely" in general terms, though by no means unimportant; on the contrary, its very dissociation from the prevailing spirit of the age enabled it to fulfill a spiritual, cultural, and ideological function of a magnitude which can hardly be exaggerated: it stood for an alternative world. The

2. R. Wagner, *Gesammelte Schriften und Dichtungen*, ed. W. Golther (Berlin and Leipzig, n.d.), 3:273ff., 282ff.

3. W. Niemann, *Die Musik seit Richard Wagner* (Berlin, 1913); E. Bücken, *Die Musik des 19. Jahrhunderts bis zur Moderne* (Wildpark-Potsdam, 1929).

saying "music is different" formed the nucleus of the musical aesthetic of an age of positivism.

Neither realism nor the spirit of the early years (the *"Gründerjahre"*) of the new German empire proclaimed in 1871, neither naturalism nor symbolism had any effect on the major musical works of the second half of the nineteenth century, with a few exceptions that did not influence style in general. This is not to deny the underlying realism of Mussorgsky's *Boris Godunov*, analogous to that of the great Russian novels, or the homage paid by the French Symbolists to Wagner. (It is hard, in any case, to agree on just what their homage has to tell us about Wagner, or on whether it related to music and musical drama at all, or primarily to the "artistic phenomenon": to the energy Wagner brought to asserting and establishing the highest cultural claims for music.) But in spite of certain affinities it is hardly possible to describe realism or symbolism as musical movements, let alone as periods in music history. Naturalism was alien and even hostile to music (the champions of art for the scientific age distrusted music, which was an invitation to romantic musing of the kind dismissed by Brecht as "gawking" [*glotzen*]). If some of the sets designed for the festival theater in Bayreuth are reminiscent of the style of Makart, it by no means signifies that Wagner's music breathes the spirit (if that is the right word for it) of the new German empire—in spite of the theory of the "total artwork," the *"Gesamtkunstwerk,"* which did not eliminate the lack of synchronism between the separate arts which were necessary to the stage realization of the drama.

Definitions of a period in the history of music or any of the other arts are never completely independent of value judgments: aesthetic decisions are made about which works belong to history (instead of merely to the debris of the past) and which not. The existence of analogies to Wagnerian music drama in some works of dubious literary merit—the products of a Wilhelm Jordan or a Felix Dahn—makes little or no difference to the gulf between the music of the late nineteenth century and its literature and painting. The quality of works representing a particular stylistic trend is of no less importance in forming a historical judgment than the number of works representing the style, or the fact that a style manifests itself in one art and not at all in another. Charpentier's *Louise* is too weak a work to stand for naturalism in music: to all intents and purposes, apart from certain elements in program music, there is no such thing. Mussorgsky's *Boris Godunov* is a major work, yet the musical realism of which it is the outstanding document is so isolated a phenomenon that it can hardly be called a style— for one of the characteristics of a style is recurrence in more than one work. The central trends of the age were represented in music by peripheral works, while the central musical works were representative of the periphery of the age.

3

The positivist age in which musical neo-romanticism had to assert itself—as the prototype of an "alternative world"— was not the same thing as the "prosaic" everyday world that oppressed the poets and composers of the early nineteenth century. The principal difference was that positivism was by no means merely the day-to-day, trivial reality to which philosophy and art could be contrasted, as constituting a "true reality"; in the early years of the century philosophy regarded itself as the quintessence of "science" precisely when it was speculative, and art was imbued with metaphysical dignity. Positivism, however, was not merely a contrast, a foil, to the spiritual, intellectual, and cultural trends of the age: it was itself the spirit of a scientific age.

Around 1800 the ideas with which music was imbued were related to the principles which were uppermost in the literature, the painting, the philosophy, and the history writing of the age. The world that existed outside this realm of culture was "prosaic." But after the middle of the century music, in which something of romanticism lived on, was the odd art out in a cultural climate that was predominantly anti-romantic. Romantic—"neo-romantic"—music found itself isolated in an age when literature and painting abhorred "ideas" (impressionism was still realism, even if it employed different techniques); when historians, after the eclipse of Hegelianism, shrank from writing speculative history; when the prevalent mode of thought among educated people increasingly reflected the methodology of the natural sciences; and when philosophy alternated between moods of positivism and metaphysics: between anxious dependency on the exact sciences on the one hand and experimental forays into "mythology" on the other. Of course some writers, painters, and historians continued to produce works tinged with romanticism, but these could not compare in significance with contemporary romantic music, which was the "great music" of the age.

Thus music increased its influence because it was almost alone in bearing the burden of providing an alternative to the realities of the world following the Industrial Revolution. (Lyric poetry of any significance had taken off into esotericism; the poetry that the general public actually read partook of neo-romanticism, but could not aspire to the heights reached by the style in music.) On the other hand, because of its alienation from the positivist zeitgeist, music could not lay claim to being a "representative" art, the document and reflection of its age. The reason why people followed Schopenhauer (who had to wait for true recognition until the second half of the century) in attributing metaphysical meaning to music was that they no longer believed that metaphysics had any true significance for reality—"true reality" now being synonymous with material reality. Music was raised to a status of incommensurability—and could then safely be ignored as irrelevant.

But music's position vis-à-vis the industrial age was not only that of a consolatory and elevating alternative to materialism: in another way they were also dialectically reconciled. Wagner himself provided the most drastic formulation of the matter in 1851, in *Opera and Drama*, when, in addition to apostrophizing Berlioz as a "neo-romantic," he called him the musical "savior" of an age of "industrial machinery." If one ignores the scornful and denunciatory tone and concentrates on what his words describe, they could easily be applied to the composer of the Magic Fire music.

> We understand now the supernatural wonders with which the priesthood used to deceive childlike people into believing that some god manifested himself to them; there was always some mechanical contrivance behind these marvels.

Wagner the mythologist, Nietzche's "sorcerer," appropriates here the thesis of "priestly deception."

> In exactly the same way nowadays the *super*natural, being as it is the *un*natural, is paraded before the bemused public solely through the marvels of machinery, and truly Berlioz's orchestra is a miracle of that order. Berlioz has explored the highest and the lowest extremities of this machinery and has thus developed a truly remarkable knowledge of its capabilities, and if we acknowledge the inventors of today's industrial machinery as benefactors of the citizens of the modern state, then we must acclaim Berlioz as the true savior of our world of absolute music

—by "absolute" Wagner meant "unmotivated": if music had no foundation in dance or words it lacked inner justification; he did not accept a program as a valid aesthetic *raison d'être* for a piece—

> for by the use of an unprecedented variety of purely mechanical means he has enabled musicians to create the most marvellous effects, even if the content of what they are playing is inartistic rubbish.[4]

The feeling that metaphysical effects in music result from mechanical causes had already troubled Wackenroder more than half a century earlier, when he formulated an aesthetics of music in the early days of romanticism.[5] But the

4. Wagner, *Gesammelte Schriften*, 3:283.
5. W. H. Wackenroder, *Werke und Briefe* (Heidelberg, 1967), pp. 205 ("Die Wunder der Tonkunst"), 220 ("Das eigentümliche innere Wesen der Tonkunst").

composer's craft of which Wackenroder was thinking had become a technique (even a technology) in the music of Berlioz—and in the music of Wagner. (The distinction Wagner chose to make between his own "motivated" dramatic music and Berlioz's "unmotivated" programmatic music is not a good enough reason to withhold from him the judgment he passed on Berlioz.) The advances in musical techniques—"advances" is an expression normally frowned upon in the writing of music history, but it is the *mot juste* here—were the precise correlative in the nineteenth century to the increase in romantic illusionism that T. W. Adorno described as "phantasmagoria."[6]

Throughout the age of scientific positivism between 1850 and 1890, coinciding with the rise and establishment of the new German empire, music was at once "untimely," inasmuch as it was still a romantic art, and a spiritual force of incalculable influence, inasmuch as it was the expression of an alternative culture. The special position of music was what enabled Wagner—whose authority as a writer on the philosophy of culture derived from his authority as a musician—to mediate between the romanticism of the early part of the century, of which he was the heir, and the *"Kulturkritik"* of the end of the century,[7] which he inspired. It was from that "critical re-evaluation of an entire culture" that a literary and philosophical neo-romanticism was born around 1900, reflecting musical neo-romanticism.

There is no mistaking the mark Wagner left on his time, yet its nature is hard to define since it manifested itself—unlike Hegelianism—less in a system of categories than in vague but powerful currents of feeling and in slogans which gave the currents an eruptive rather than a rationally comprehensible expression. (Terms like *"das Allgemein-menschliche"*—meaning "that which is common to all mankind," "the general human lot"—or formulas like

6. T. W. Adorno, *Versuch über Wagner* (Frankfurt am Main, 1952), pp. 107ff.

7. E. Troeltsch, "Das Neunzehnte Jahrhundert," in *Gesammelte Schriften*, vol. 4 (Tübingen, 1925), pp. 614–49.

the postulate that music should be the means of "realizing the poetic intention for the feelings" are as fundamental to Wagner's thinking as their meaning is hazy to someone who tries to analyze them dispassionately without being swept along in the Wagnerian current.)

The actual texts of Wagner's writings on the philosophy of culture did not exert a very great influence, nor were the ideas he expressed in his writings automatically taken seriously out of deference to his musical authority. It was the music itself which had an effect on the philosophy of culture. We could, with only a tinge of exaggeration, speak of the "cultural re-evaluation" of the end of the century as being born from the spirit of music—Wagner's music. But his own writings constituted only one—and not the decisive one—among several attempts to interpret the significance of his music for the philosophy of culture.

4

If Wagner's was the dominant, so to speak "official," music of the second half of the nineteenth century—and the most partisan adherents of Brahms, those who regarded Wagner's later works as a dreadful omen for the future of music, did not deny that they were a phenomenon overshadowing everything else—at the same time, and not by chance, "unofficial," "trivial" music evolved to become a musico-psychological force such as it had not been before. We can see here a qualitative leap in the development of "low" (as opposed to "high") art. The paradoxical intermingling (typical of Germany in the 1870s) of two contrary and apparently mutually exclusive tendencies—of the positivism which regarded itself as the spirit of an industrial age, and of a neo-romanticism which was out of its proper time and yet powerful—is as clearly illustrated by the products of the musical basement as by the "great art" produced on the *piano nobile.*

The fact that musical neo-romanticism was a late flowering of romanticism in a positivist age—without being epigonal in any derogatory sense—was one of the aesthetic circumstances that shaped and encouraged the spread of musical kitsch in the second half of the nineteenth century (The decisive social cause, which would have been as ineffectual without the aesthetic factor as the aesthetic factor would have been without the social cause, was of course the desire of the classes made prosperous by the political and social circumstances of the age to have their own form of the bourgeois musical culture that was shaped by romantic tradition.)

Musical kitsch, whether rousing and high-flown or soothingly sentimental, is a decadent form of romantic music. When the *noble simplicité* of a classical style descends to the market place, the result is banality—the mere husks of classical forms—but hardly ever kitsch. Kitsch in music has hybrid ambitions which far outreach the capabilities of its actual structures and sounds, and are manifested in effects without cause, empty attitudinizing, and titles and instructions for performance which are not justified by the musical results. Instead of being content with modest achievements within its reach, musical kitsch has pretensions to big emotions, to "significance," and these are rooted in what are still recognizably romantic preconceptions, however depraved.

Another thing which has always led to works being branded as kitsch is the sense that they are somehow mechanical, calculated, "manufactured." In other circumstances, an aesthetic theory that disparages the "making," the construction—the *poiein* that gives poetry its name—may itself be open to question and alien to art; but in the case of kitsch it hits the nail on the head. How a piece of musical kitsch is made, put together, is particularly obvious, even if only to listeners who are capable of hearing musical structures at all, because it is primitive; and since kitsch subscribes to the anti-mannerist principle, common to both romantic and classical art, that artifice must be concealed in art, its primitive construction contradicts and undermines its aesthetic intentions. Its pretensions to emotional immediacy collapse when the listener is able to see through its calculation. The "industrial machinery" to which Wagner discovered a musical analogy in the orchestral technique of Berlioz—a machinery central to neo-romantic music as a whole, giving it its particular characteristics of a romantic art that employed the means of a positivist, industrial age—is thus also at work in musical kitsch, but—and the distinction is crucial—it is employed schematically. The Magic Fire declines into pyrotechnics. The decisive point aesthetically is not, as the adherents of a sentimental, popular, aesthetic theory believe, the sincerity or insincerity of the emotions expressed in the music. For one thing, sincerity is a questionable aesthetic category, and for another, no one has the moral right to impugn the sincerity of the emotions that give rise to kitsch. What is decisive is the sheer inadequacy of the machinery, its rudimentary schematics, its spurious invention.

As decadent romanticism (typical of the age in that respect), kitsch makes us aware of one element which threatens all the music of the later nineteenth century, the great neo-romantic art as well as the trivial pseudo-romantic art, and that is the "untimeliness" of romantic attitudes and ways of thought. Of course neo-romantic music of quality does not raise the aesthetic objections that apply to the kitsch of the same era: there is no disparity between its expressive character and its compositional techniques—the "poetic intention" and its "realization," as Wagner would say. But it is dogged by the awareness, or at the very least by an obscure presentiment, that the romanticism to which it holds fast—or of which it is the fulfillment, as Wagner's champions claim for the founder of Bayreuth—is no longer "substantial" (in the objective, historico-philosophical sense, not the subjective, psychological sense; it is not its sincerity that is in question, but its historical authenticity).

The loss of historico-philosophical substance emerges aesthetically in the fact that it is impossible to give romantic intentions a simple direct expression. In the first half of the century profound and significant thought could legiti-

mately be expressed in straightforward musical language,
inasmuch as directness and simplicity were in accord with
the romantic zeitgeist. But in the second half of the century
such a mode of expression at once came under the suspicion
of being kitsch (and since aesthetic cases are tried by public
opinion, not by learned judges, suspicion is already tan-
tamount to conviction). Therefore, if it was not to sink to
basement level, musical neo-romanticism had to have re-
course to complex compositional techniques (such as lie behind the apparently artless simplicity of *Die Meistersinger*),
that is, to the "industrial machinery" of a Berlioz that
aroused Wagner to simultaneous admiration and denuncia-
tion. The "machinery," in other words the deployment of
musical technology (as opposed to musical craftsmanship, of
which Wagner and Berlioz were considered not fully masters
by some of their contemporaries, and not always those who
were the worst judges), though it is in one respect a document of the spirit of the industrial, positivist age, is not so
much a denial of the neo-romantic "poetic intention" as an
essential factor in its musical realization. It is the artistic
quality of the realization which distinguishes it from kitsch,
which cannot bridge the gulf between its primitive techniques and its "poetic" pretensions.

5

The attempt to understand the musical neo-romanticism of
the second half of the nineteenth century as romantic art in
an unromantic, positivist age presupposes something which
is by no means self-evident, namely that the decades between 1850 and 1890 (or 1910) form a coherent epoch, distinct from romanticism on one side and modernism (or the
"new music") on the other. (The period around 1900
thought of and referred to itself as "modern.")
　　Some music historians are inclined to place less stress on
the caesura of circa 1850 and more on the end of classicism
and early romanticism around 1830, and to regard the "musical revolution" of circa 1910 as the end of the romantic

age, rather than the changes that took place around 1890.[8]
The differences are due not so much to varying opinions
about facts and circumstances as to divergences in the underlying historiographic principles.

The year 1830 seems an obvious place for the caesura if
Berlioz is contrasted with Beethoven and Meyerbeer with
Rossini, and if events in France are placed in the forefront:
the end of the Bourbon restoration, which in music was Rossini's heyday, and the establishment of the July monarchy,
as whose musical representatives Wagner coupled Berlioz
and Meyerbeer.[9] In Germany, on the other hand, the relationship between Weber and the young Wagner (the composer of "romantic operas," which it is willful to reinterpret
as "music dramas"), or that between Beethoven and
Schubert on the one hand (as Thrasybulos Georgiades has
shown, early romanticism and Viennese classicism inter-
mingle[10]) and Schumann and Mendelssohn on the other, is
too close to allow talk of two ages or the end of a musical era.
(Schumann was no musical Heine; rather, the German
romantics after 1830 regarded themselves, with some justice, as the heirs of Beethoven, the executors of the musical
testament that Beethoven had left in his late works.) Thus
the importance of 1830 for the music historian depends on
whether he considers the relationship music bore to events
and structural changes in the political and social arena more
or less decisive than the aesthetic standing music reached
on its own, as an autonomous art. In other words, it depends
on whether he chooses to draw his musico-historical frontiers according to the major events in political and social
history (in which France was the leader) in spite of the relatively weak impression those events made on music, or
according to the major events in music history (in which

8. F. Blume, "Die Musik von 1830 bis 1914: Strukturprobleme einer
Epoche," in Kongressbericht Kassel 1962, pp. 40–50.

9. Wagner, Gesammelte Schriften, 3:300.

10. T. G. Georgiades, Schubert, Musik und Lyrik (Göttingen, 1967), pp.
127ff.

Germany was the leader) precisely because the impact of political and social events was relatively slight.

Estimation of the alternative claim of 1850 to be the
proper place for a musico-historical caesura is tied up with
the methodological decision as to whether emphasis should
fall on musical style—understood as the essence of musical
means—or on the meaning music had in the contemporary
consciousness. The stylistic continuity between Schumann
and Brahms, Berlioz and Liszt, the Wagner of the romantic
operas and the Wagner of the music dramas, may be seen as
grounds for designating the entire century "romantic" so far
as its music is concerned, so that the caesuras of circa 1850
and circa 1890 diminish in importance to the level of divi-
sions between phases of romanticism. Alternatively, the decisive factor may seem to be the historico-philosophical distinction between romanticism and neo-romanticism—the
gulf between musical romanticism in a romantic age and
musical neo-romanticism in a positivist age. The difference
of opinions is less important, however, than the insight into
the premises that support each of the differing opinions, and
into the relative extent to which each can be said to be right.

The central political event of the mid-century was the
revolution of 1848–9. That a virtually simultaneous caesura
or turning-point can also be seen in music history cannot
however be explained by a simple attribution of musical
events to socio-historical causes. Wagner's romantic operas
(*Der fliegende Holländer, Tannhäuser* and *Lohengrin*) and
some of Liszt's major works were written before 1850, and it
would be wrong to deny the continuity between the pre-
1850 and post-1850 works of both composers for the sake of
a thesis. Yet stylistic changes patently did take place,[11] and
there is no mistaking the altered "tone" of music after 1850:
it became either forced or resigned, as though, for all the
continued adherence to the romantic idea, the idea had lost
its substance. The composers who died within a few years of
1850—Mendelssohn, Schumann, Chopin—represent a dif-

11. H. Rietsch, *Die Tonkunst in der zweiten Hälfte des neunzehnten
Jahrhunderts* (Leipzig, 1900).

ferent era from that of Wagner and Liszt, although they belong to the same generation. (The operas Wagner wrote before 1850 can be seen as forerunners of his later music
dramas in certain respects, but if Schumann had lived to
Wagner's age it is unlikely that he would have done anything more than repeat himself; the decisive factor is not
that he died but that, by 1850, unlike Wagner's, his work
was done.)

It is not easy, however, to express unambiguously in a few
words the connection between the 1848–9 revolution and
its consequences and the musical innovations of the early
1850s: aesthetically, the change in the significance of music
indicated by the word neo-romanticism; in the history of
genres, the establishment of music drama by Wagner and of
the symphonic poem by Liszt. The relationship between the
musical changes and the political and social events and
trends is ambivalent. It is obvious on the one hand that the
revolution and its failure had an immense influence on
Wagner's conception and shaping of the *Ring,* the paradigm
of music drama; not only the subject of the drama was affected but the character of the music as well. On the other
hand, while the compositional techniques of the symphonic
poems Liszt wrote in the 1850s are undoubtedly representative of the "new music" of their time—the "music of the
future"—their spiritual and intellectual structures were essentially informed by the French romanticism of the 1830s,
to whose ideas and attitudes Liszt remained unshakably
loyal, passé though they were by 1850. (Even his attitude
towards the German classicism that he systematically up-
held in Weimar was conditioned by French romanticism's
view of classicism.)

The caesura that can be drawn around 1890, the start of
the era of "modernism," is marked in the political field by
the "new imperialism" of the late nineteenth century,[12] and
in intellectual and cultural history by the "cultural re-

12. G. Barraclough, *Tendenzen der Geschichte im 20. Jahrhundert*
(Munich, 1967) [*An Introduction to Contemporary History*, London 1964],
I. §3.

evaluation" of the turn of the century.[13] It would be absurd to draw a direct analogy between the musical modernism of the 1890s, whose standard-bearers were Strauss and Mahler (primarily Strauss and secondly Mahler in the eyes of their contemporaries, the other way round in the view of posterity), and the political and philosophical trends of the time—that is, to regard musical innovations merely as a reflection of events outside music. All the same, the spirit of cultural re-evaluation undoubtedly affected thinking about music. Profound changes were taking place virtually simultaneously in different arenas, political and social as well as musical, and that is a fact that positively incites to historico-philosophical speculation, even if materialist reductionism may be regarded with as much distrust as idealist reductionism, because the former seems to be only the latter stood on its head, a negative yet dependent variant of it.

13. Troeltsch, "Neunzehnte Jahrhundert," pp. 641ff.

The Twofold Truth in Wagner's Aesthetics: Nietzsche's Fragment "On Music and Words"

❦

1

Friedrich Nietzsche's fragment "On Music and Words" ("Über Musik und Wort")[1] probably dates from 1871 and seems likely to have originated either as a section of *The Birth of Tragedy* which he decided to omit on publication, or as part of a projected book on ancient Greece which he never completed.[2] At all events—assuming that the dating is not out by half a decade, and its subject matter precludes so great a miscalculation—it was written at a time when Nietzsche's friendship with Wagner was still unclouded. This makes all the more remarkable the implicit polemic against some of the fundamental theses of Wagner's aesthetic theory, a polemic delivered in a tone which is given an offensive edge by Nietzsche's customary manner of taking for granted the meretriciousness of whatever he was arguing against. The fragment is one of the testimonies to his

1. F. Nietzsche, "Über Musik und Wort" (hereafter referred to as "Fragment"), in *Sprache, Dichtung, Musik*, ed. J. Knaus (Tübingen, 1973), pp. 20–32; English renderings of passages from the "Fragment" in this essay are by Walter Kaufmann, whose version of the entire "Fragment" is reprinted in the Appendix—all other translation is my own [*Translator*].

2. L. Rohner, *Deutsche Essays* (Munich, 1972), 3:215.

19

enthusiasm for all things Wagnerian, and yet it contains the outlines of his later critique of Wagner, which culminated in his rejection of the theater as a contemptible art form, fit only for the masses.

We can discount the possibility that Nietzsche was unacquainted with *Opera and Drama*, the official handbook of Wagner's aesthetic and historical philosophy. Even if his stylistic sensibilities prevented him from reading it to the end, he must have got as far as the statement, in the introduction, of the fundamental principle: "The error in opera as a genre was that a means of expression (the music) was made the end, while the end of expression (the drama) was made a means."[3] Nietzsche must therefore have known that he was challenging and contradicting Wagner when he wrote in the fragment "On Music and Words" that it is a "strange presumption" to place music "in the service of a series of images and concepts, to use it as a means to an end, for their intensification and clarification."[4] By the "series of [visual] images and [verbal] concepts" he meant the drama, as an entity compounded of mime and speech. Music is not a means to the dramatic end, he wrote, but, on the contrary, drama is an expression and a simile or metaphor (*Gleichnis*) of music. Schopenhauer had been "absolutely right when he characterized the drama and its relation to music as a schema, as an example versus a general concept."[5] The essence of things is heard in music; drama merely reproduces their appearance. Nietzsche's polemic is not, however, directed against musical drama itself, as realized by Wagner in the *Ring* and *Tristan*, but against the theory outlined in *Opera and Drama*, which Wagner modified and qualified in later writings, though he never withdrew it. "Music never *can* become a means," Nietzsche wrote,

> however one may push, thumbscrew or torture it: as sound, as a drum roll, in its crudest and simplest stages, it still overcomes

3. Wagner, *Gesammelte Schriften*, 3:231; cf. Nietzsche, *Werke*, ed. K. Schlechta (Munich, 1966), 1:247.
4. Nietzsche, Fragment, p. 115, below.   5. Ibid., p. 107, below.

poetry and reduces it to its reflection. Opera as a genre in accordance with this concept [the concept of music as a means to a dramatic end] is thus less a perversion of music than it is an erroneous representation [*Vorstellung*] in aesthetics.[6]

According to *Opera and Drama* the function of musical expression is to "realize the poetic intention for the feelings": to present the creative artist's initial and underlying idea not merely to the intellect or understanding but directly to a region of perception where instinct and the emotions together recognize the truth in the evidence presented by the senses. It was only with such "realization" that drama becomes drama at all for Wagner.

> If the poetic intention is still discernible as such it is because it has not been fully subsumed, that is, realized, in the composer's expression; on the other hand, if the composer's expression is still recognizable as such it is because it has not been completely permeated by the poetic intention; only when the expression has surrendered its individual, particular identity in the realization of that intention, do both intention and expression cease to exist, and the reality to which both aspired is achieved: that reality is the drama, in the performance of which we should no longer be conscious of either intention or expression, because we are overwhelmed by its content, as an expression of which we instinctively acknowledge the necessary human truth.[7]

Nietzsche is contemptuous of the "poetic intention," in which, according to Wagner, the musical drama originates. "But how should the image, the representation be capable of generating music? Not to speak of the notion that the concept or, as has been said, the 'poetical idea' should be capable of doing this!"[8] Poetic ideas are not the foundation of music; music is the foundation of poetic ideas. What appears to come first, the text, is in point of fact second—not only metaphysically but even genetically: "a musical excitement that comes from altogether different regions *chooses*" a text

6. Ibid., p. 116, below.
7. Wagner, *Gesammelte Schriften*, 4:207.
8. Nietzsche, Fragment, p. 109, below.

to be "a metaphorical expression for itself."⁹ And where
music presents itself undiminished as that which it really is,
metaphors or similes are superfluous and distracting.

> Confronted with the supreme revelations of music, we even
> feel, willy-nilly, the *crudeness* of all imagery and of every emo-
> tion that might be adduced by way of an analogy. Thus Beetho-
> ven's last quartets put to shame everything visual and the whole
> realm of empirical reality.[10]

Nietzsche's verdict on hermeneutic "crudeness" calls involuntarily to mind Wagner's programmatic interpretation
of Beethoven's C♯ minor Quartet op. 131 in his 1870 essay
on the composer[11] (with which Nietzsche was undoubtedly
familiar, since he explicitly quotes from it in "On Music and
Words"[12]). The nineteenth century's exegetical zeal produced innumerable examples of musical works being treated
as if they were chapters of autobiography; Wagner's program
for op. 131 differs in being prefaced by the explanation that
his interpretation of it as the "depiction of a day in the life of
our saint" is intended only in an "analogical," not an "identifying," sense, and that readers will not recognize the
merits of the interpretation so much while actually listening to the music—for in the immediate experience of it
music is a "revelation from another world"—but when they
are reflecting on the music after hearing it. Thus Wagner
both offers the program and at the same time half withdraws
it: which is characteristic of the way his later writings prop-
agate not one but two aesthetic truths.

In the choral finale of Beethoven's Ninth Symphony
orchestral music, for inherent musical reasons, makes a
transition into vocal music: Wagner's historico-philosophical thesis that it was the "last symphony,"[13] and signified
the end of absolute music (music that was absolute in sub-

---

9. Ibid., p. 112, below.   10. Ibid., p. 112, below.
11. Wagner, *Gesammelte Schriften*, 9:96f.
12. Nietzsche, Fragment, p. 113, below.
13. Wagner, *Gesammelte Schriften*, 3:97 (*Das Kunstwerk der Zukunft*).

stance) provoked Nietzsche to riposte in a scornful tone which is astonishing in an utterance of 1871, the time of his friendship with Wagner.

> What, then, are we to say of the incredible aesthetic superstition that Beethoven in the fourth movement of the "Ninth" gave a solemn testimony concerning the limits of absolute music and thus unlocked the portals to a new art in which music is said to be able to represent even images and concepts and has thus supposedly been made accessible for "conscious spirit"?[14]

It is possible that Nietzsche's polemic—the scorn he expresses for the "conscious spirit," which is led by an aesthetic error to think itself superior to the unconscious impulses of an earlier age—was directed not so much against Wagner as against Franz Brendel, who shared Wagner's views about the "end of the symphony,"[15] for it was Brendel who tried repeatedly, with the persistence of the dogmatist, the ideologist of a musical faction, to make a distinction between earlier "instinctive" composition and modern "conscious" composition.[16] (The thesis that, as Nietzsche puts it, music "is able to represent even images and concepts" served Brendel, though not Wagner, as the justification, aesthetically and historico-philosophically, of the program music of Berlioz and Liszt.) On the other hand it is a fact that Wagner too praised the finale of the Ninth Symphony as the sign and the paradigm of a transition to "conscious" composition: "With this melody [Freude, schöner Götterfunken] music's mystery is solved for us: now we know, we have won the ability to be artists who can create organically in full consciousness."[17] ("Creating organically with consciousness" meant being conscious of music's foundation in poetry as a condition of organic, as opposed to mechanical, composition.)

14. Nietzsche, Fragment, p. 113, below.
15. F. Brendel, *Geschichte der Musik in Italien, Deutschland und Frankreich*, 4th ed. (Leipzig, 1867), p. 593; cf. also pp. 355f.
16. Ibid., pp. 594, 597f., 634.
17. Wagner, *Gesammelte Schriften*, 3:312 (*Oper und Drama*).

2

One of the central elements in Nietzsche's later critique of Wagner, his disparagement of the theater, is already prefigured in "On Music and Words" without its polemic potential yet being apparent. Both in the essay on Beethoven, which was fresh in Nietzsche's mind when he was writing in 1871, and in *Opera and Drama* twenty years earlier, Wagner stressed the importance of the mimetic and scenic elements in musical drama.

> We know that the lines written by a poet, even a Goethe or a Schiller, cannot determine music; only drama can do that, and by drama I mean not the dramatic poem or text but the drama we see taking place before our eyes, the visible reflection of the music, where the words and utterances belong solely to the action, and no longer to the poetic idea.[18]

Verbal utterance—*parola scenica* as Verdi called it—forms just one of the elements in a theatrical action, but it is the action as a whole which gives reality to the poetic idea by enabling it to reach the emotions and senses directly, instead of its merely being enunciated for the intellect to receive.

The sentence from Wagner's *Beethoven* quoted in the previous paragraph is equivocal in its description of the relationship between music and drama, for on the one hand drama is said to be able to "determine music," but on the other hand it is presented as the "visible reflection of the music": "das sichtbar gewordenes Gegenbild der Musik," a use of Schopenhauer's terminology which implicitly concedes that the music is the *"Urbild,"* the "original" of the reflected image. Priority is split between music and drama—both determine and simultaneously both are determined; when Nietzsche puts the mimetic and scenic elements into second place, in the 1871 fragment, he is confronting an earlier product of Wagnerian aesthetic theory, the principal thesis of *Opera and Drama,* with a more recent

18. Ibid., 9:111f. (*Beethoven*).

theory, which Wagner formed under the influence of Schopenhauer. What is one half of the aesthetic truth proclaimed by Wagner, that the drama, the theatrical action, is a "reflection" of the music, a "deed of music that has become visible,"[19] is the whole truth for Nietzsche, and he expresses it with polemical directness.

> Opera in this sense, of course, is at best good music and only music, while the imposture that goes on at the same time is, so to say, merely a fantastic disguise of the orchestra, and, above all, of its most important instruments, the singers, something on which people of insight turn their backs, laughing.[20]

The contempt for the theater, for stage spectacle, which Nietzsche expressed with ever increasing vehemence in his later critique of Wagner, is latent in Wagner's own aesthetic theory, insofar as it is based on Schopenhauer. Nietzsche put into words what he had himself experienced while watching *Tristan*, when he wrote:

> ... for at every point where the Dionysian power of the music strikes the listener like lightning, the eyes that behold the action and were absorbed in the individuals appearing before us become moist, and the listener *forgets* the drama and wakes up again for it only after the Dionysian spell is broken.[21]

This passage owes rather more to Wagner than the experience it describes: although it contradicts the earlier stratum of Wagner's aesthetic theory and thus implies a criticism of Wagner, it is very nearly a quotation of Wagner's own words from *Beethoven* ("gesture" [*Gebärde*] is Wagner's shorthand term for the mimetic and scenic aspects of the action as a whole):

> Music expresses the innermost essence of gesture with such immediate comprehensibility that, once it has completely filled our beings, it diminishes even the power of our sight to concen-

19. Ibid., 9:306 (*Über die Benennung "Musikdrama"*).
20. Nietzsche, Fragment, p. 117, below.
21. Ibid., pp. 117f., below.

trate on the gesture, so that finally we understand it without even seeing it.[22]

"The drama we see taking place before our eyes"—the ultimate aesthetic authority in *Opera and Drama*—was still important to Wagner in 1870, but by then he was no longer in the planning stages of the *Ring*. By then he had written *Tristan*, and he admitted the subjection of the drama to the superior power of the music.

Thus the fragment "On Music and Words" contains the elements of a critique of Wagner which Nietzsche, by adroit, selective emphasis, was able to derive directly from Wagner's own aesthetic theory and the twofold truth it contained.

Wagner himself, in an outburst of disgust with the "business of costumes and make-up," once said in 1878 that he wished he could invent "invisible theater";[23] Nietzsche accused him, in *The Case of Wagner*, of having brought about the "decline of art" and the "demoralization" of the artist by the "total transformation of art into theatrical spectacle."[24] He depicted Wagner's "theatrical genius" as bringing a historical—or historico-philosophical—doom in its wake. In *Nietzsche contra Wagner* he wrote: "You can see that my nature is intrinsically anti-theatrical, in the very depths of my soul I feel that profound contempt for the theater, the mass art par excellence, that every artist feels today."[25] "We know the masses, we know the theater."[26] Though Nietzsche celebrated the first Bayreuth festival, in the fourth of the *Thoughts out of Season* ("Richard Wagner in Bayreuth") in 1876, as a repudiation of the modern theater exemplified by the Paris Opéra,[27] he later, after his "conversion," denounced the festivals as a manifestation and a symptom of the very ruin they had been intended to avert.

22. Wagner, *Gesammelte Schriften*, 9:77; cf. also 9:104.
23. C. F. Glasenapp, *Das Leben Richard Wagners*, vol. 6 (Leipzig, 1911), pp. 137f.
24. Nietzsche, *Werke*, 2:916.
25. Ibid., 2:1041.   26. Ibid., 2:914.   27. Ibid., 1:410.

With the scorn that is nourished by former admiration, Nietzsche emphasized Wagner's "histrionic" side, something he equated with "inauthenticity."[28] The category of inauthenticity was later taken to apply only to the psychology of individual artists and adopted in that form by a school of aestheticians, to the detriment of aesthetics. But in Nietzsche it is a central charge, which he levelled by no means solely at Wagner, but at the modern theater as a whole, and therefore it was not intended primarily as a psychological aspersion. If the argument is not simply to provoke the trite counter-argument that it is a waste of time to blame the theater for being theatrical instead of being an immediate expression of psychological reality, it has to be understood metaphysically. Closer analysis shows that once again Nietzsche was making polemical capital out of the dichotomy in Wagner's aesthetic theories.

The fundamental thesis of *Opera and Drama*, that music must be a means at the service of drama—"the drama we see taking place before our eyes," that is, the stage action—was turned inside out by Nietzsche (as if he had forgotten his *Tristan* experience) and used to attack Wagner—the composer, not just the theorist—on the grounds that, in the creation of his musical dramas, Wagner denied music's metaphysical primacy and made mimetic and scenic elements his starting point, gave priority to his theatrical intuition. "Wagner starts with a hallucination, not of sounds but of gestures. Then he looks about him for a semiotic in sound with which to express them."[29] In order to prove his charge that Wagner was first and foremost a theatrical showman, who also happened to compose, Nietzsche takes up Wagner's own anticipatory description of his own work in *Opera and Drama* (the fallibility of which Nietzsche ought really to have learned from his own *Tristan* experience) and demolishes it by the use of critical categories based on Schopenhauer's metaphysics of music, that is, on an aes-

28. Ibid., 2:919, 925.   29. Ibid., 2:917.

thetic philosophy which owed its pre-eminence in the later nineteenth century entirely to its adoption by Wagner. Not that the genesis of Nietzsche's polemic makes any difference to its validity or lack thereof. (There is no contradiction between doubting whether any definite conclusions can be drawn at all over the genetic priority of music or staging in Wagner's creative processes, and simultaneously believing that psychological genesis and aesthetic validity need not coincide, that is, that the priority of the mimetic and scenic "hallucination" in the genesis of a work does not rule out the aesthetic and metaphysical primacy of the music.) It is of some importance, however, that Nietzsche reformulated Wagner's aesthetic theory in such a way as to turn the dialectical relationship between the two truths it contained (a relationship which will be analyzed closely below) into one of contradiction, in order to fuel an ambiguous polemic, in which revulsion was mingled with enthusiasm. (In 1876, in the panegyric *Richard Wagner in Bayreuth*, Nietzsche was still able to discuss elements that later were to disgust him—"theater," "effect," "mass art"—in a neutral tone, not exactly enthusiastic but without any perceptible intrinsic hostility:

> When the dominating idea of his [Wagner's] life rose up in him, the idea that an incomparable effect, an effect greater than that of any other art, could be exercised by the theater, it stirred his being into the most violent ferment.[30]

He also referred to Wagner's "primal theatrical gift"[31] without any suggestion of a sneer, without any of that disparagement of histrionic talent which in any case was at odds with his admiration for Aeschylus.)

3

Schopenhauer's metaphysics of the "will" was modified by Nietzsche in the fragment "On Music and Words" by a process of subdividing concepts which at first sight may appear to be a grave infringement of the rule that concepts should

30. Ibid., 1:402.   31. Ibid., 1:398.

not be multiplied unnecessarily. The purpose of it becomes clear only when it is seen to be a means of making metaphysical provisions with which to solve aesthetic problems. Metaphysics is being used as an organon of aesthetics, instead of aesthetics being, as Schelling put it, an organon of metaphysics.

The "will," Schopenhauer's ultimate authority, is, according to Nietzsche, "nothing but the most general manifestation of something that is otherwise totally indecipherable for us"[32] a likeness, that is, not the original image—a "general manifestation," not the "thing in itself." On the other hand Nietzsche distinguishes between the "will"— the "basic ground of pleasure and displeasure"[33] which lies beneath all the stirrings of the soul and the processes of the conscious mind—and feeling, the mere emotions and instincts, which are "already permeated and saturated by conscious and unconscious representations";[34] which have, that is, moved further from the "indecipherable."

In Schopenhauer's metaphysics of music the "will," representing both the music's content and its origins, was equated with feeling, but Nietzsche subdivides this basic concept into no fewer than three categories: the "indecipherable," the "will," and the emotions. He defines the "indecipherable" as the "origin" of music, the "will" as its "subject," and the emotions as a mere "symbol": music is not the likeness and expression of an emotion, the emotion is a metaphor of the music.[35] Schopenhauer was not above adopting from popular aesthetics the proposition that music is an "imageless language of the heart,"[36] but Nietzsche was roused to combat the "corrupt emotional theory of aesthetics," as Hanslick called it.[37] "Feeling . . . is altogether the inartistic *par excellence* in the realm of creative art, and

32. Nietzsche, Fragment, p. 108, below.

33. Ibid., p. 110, below.   34. Ibid., p. 111, below.

35. Ibid., p. 111, below.

36. A. Schopenhauer, *Parerga und Paralipomena*, §224 ("Zur Metaphysik des Schönen"), quoted by Nietzsche, Fragment, p. 106, below.

37. E. Hanslick, *Vom Musikalisch-Schönen* (1854; modern reprint, Darmstadt, 1965), p. v (preface).

only its total exclusion makes possible the full self-absorption of the artist and his disinterested contemplation."[38] From this it seems that Nietzsche has adopted the maxim that works of art are not created in the full flood of emotion but require contemplative distance. On the other hand he sees the origins of music lying in the "indecipherable," something that he understands to be a "power," "that in the form of the 'will' generates a visionary world: the origin of music lies beyond all individuation."[39] The relationship between the "indecipherable" and the artist's "disinterested contemplation"—or between the "Dionysian" and the "Apollinian," in the language of *The Birth of Tragedy*—remains undefined. But it is clear that Nietzsche, unlike Schopenhauer, disowned the emotional theory of aesthetics: emotions do not provide music with underlying premises or expressive content, but are merely a simile into which music can be translated. "All those who feel, when listening to music, that the music has an effect on their emotions" are concerning themselves with secondary matters. "The distant and remote power of music appeals to an intermediate realm in them, that gives them, so to say, a foretaste, a symbolical preconcept of the real music, the intermediate realm of the emotions."[40] The "real" music is "absolute" music,[41] which can have meaning without needing to be the "language of the heart."

The statement that the "will" is what forms the "subject" of music is very nearly a quotation from Schopenhauer, but the similarity of the formulations should not be allowed to disguise the differences in what they mean. For one thing, as has already been said, Nietzsche distinguishes the will, "this basic ground of pleasure and displeasure," from the emotions. Secondly the idea that this basic ground can be the subject of music, but the emotions, "already permeated and saturated by conscious and unconscious representa-

38. Nietzsche, Fragment, pp. 110, below.
39. Ibid., p. 111, below.
40. Ibid., p. 111, below.   41. Ibid., pp. 107f., below.

tions," cannot, is not very far from the thesis of Hanslick the "formalist" that music can express only the "dynamic" aspect of the emotions, but not their specific subjective nature, contingent on the conception of a particular object.[42] Thirdly, if it is emphasized that the origin of music is in the indecipherable, the result will be to remove music completely from the realm of the emotions, and to diminish the importance of the concept of the will as music's subject, because, for Nietzsche, when the origin of a thing has been determined, the essence of its being has been defined.

The musical aesthetic Nietzsche outlined in the fragment "On Words and Music" seems therefore, not to put too fine a point on it, to be a covert argument on behalf of "absolute" music, a translation of a doctrine which may seem empirical and limited when expounded by Hanslick into the language of Schopenhauerian metaphysics, which originally accepted the emotional theory of aesthetics.

4

The aesthetic of "absolute" music was expressed by Hanslick with conspicuous sobriety and with due regard to the persuasive effects of an appeal to common sense. In this guise it was carried along on the anti-Hegelian current of the age, but it was nothing other than the reformulation of a thesis that had been expounded in enthusiastic language half a century earlier by romantics such as Friedrich Schlegel and E. T. A. Hoffmann, so that the metaphysical turn given it by Nietzsche amounted to a restitution. In the "Athenäum" fragments of 1798 Schlegel, on the one hand, attributed to "pure instrumental music" a "certain tendency" towards philosophy, or philosophical meditation, and, on the other hand, dismissed the saying that music was the "language of sensibility" as the "banal point of view of so-called naturalness."[43] These were ideas that Nietzsche

42. Hanslick, *Vom Musikalisch-Schönen*, p. 14.
43. F. Schlegel, *Charakteristiken und Kritiken I*, Kritische Friedrich-Schlegel-Ausgabe, vol. 2 (Munich, 1967), p. 254.

later developed in the fragment "On Music and Words": the interpretation of "absolute" music (the term as such was unknown to Schlegel and Hoffmann) as an organon of metaphysics, or as a "premonition of the spirit realm," and the repudiation of the emotional theory of aesthetics, which belonged not so much to romanticism as to the Enlightenment and later to the Biedermeier outlook.

On the other hand, Nietzsche's development as an aesthetician depended first and foremost on his relationship with Wagner (he was hardly conscious of the connection between his modification of Schopenhauer's musical metaphysics and the romantic theory of "pure instrumental music"). And—although it may at first sound like a deliberately provocative paradox—it is perfectly reasonable to claim that, at the same time as Wagner pronounced the doctrine that music is, or ought to be, a means to a dramatic end, he also espoused other, contradictory aesthetic principles which reveal that he, hardly less than the "formalists" who were his opponents in the day-to-day cut and thrust of musical debate, took for granted the truth of the idea of an "absolute" music which was characteristic of the nineteenth century as a whole. *Opera and Drama*, officially his principal theoretical work, propagates an "exoteric" aesthetic, but there is another, "esoteric," Wagnerian theory of aesthetics, the components of which are to be found scattered throughout the later writings. It was a theory for initiates which Nietzsche took as his starting point but then carried to an extreme where it was converted into a critique of Wagner and finally into outright polemic against him.

Wagner once talked about "absolute" music—an expression that appears to have been invented by him—in a negative sense. In *The Artwork of the Future*[44] he uses the term to refer to a "pure instrumental music" which has been "released" (or "absolved" [*abgelöst*], hence "absolute") from its original motivation in dance and thereafter "desires" to be "redeemed" *(erlöst)* by a poem (as in the finale of the Ninth

Symphony) or by a drama from the unhappy isolation where
it languishes without an aesthetic raison d'être. In *Opera
and Drama*, however, he also designates such operatic
music as is not determined by and founded in drama, but
attempts instead to create drama or the appearance of drama
out of itself, as "absolute" music,[45] because it has no foundation or reason for existence. Thus Spontini is an "absolute musician,"[46] Rossini's melody is "absolute melody."[47]

As Wagner understood it, "absolute" music was deficient
(in spite of his enthusiasm for Beethoven's symphonies: the
Hegelian concept of "subjectively" admiring what you
nevertheless "objectively" rejected from the historico-
philosophical standpoint was a commonplace by 1850). The
release of melody from "the conditioning poetic substratum"[48] may mark an advance in terms of compositional
technique, but aesthetically melody is reduced, diminished.
"Unconditionality" is seen as a deficiency, a logical absurdity, not as a metaphysical distinction (as in the romantic
theory of "pure instrumental music"). And since the concept of "absolute" music is negative in its formulation—
being determined by its loss of association with language
and dance, with the extra-musical "formal motives"[49]
which lend music a "need to exist"—it can (like all negative
concepts) embrace the most extreme variety of phenomena,
from Beethoven's symphonic instrumental melodic writing
to Rossini's operatic melodic writing. "Absolute" music is
everything that Wagner wanted to separate from musical
drama, as the idea of it shaped itself in his mind around
1850.

If, in *Opera and Drama*, where he proceeded from the
thesis that music was a means to the dramatic end and nothing more, Wagner's conviction of the absurdity of "absolute" music admitted no qualifications or doubts, once he
began to read Schopenhauer in 1854 his certainty started to
waver. The question whether music, of itself, without a

45. Ibid., 3:233.   46. Ibid., 3:241.
47. Ibid., 3:251, 255.   48. Ibid., 3:276 (*Oper und Drama*).
49. Ibid., 5:191 (*Über Franz Liszts symphonische Dichtungen*).

foundation in language or dance (mimetic and scenic representation in drama was included in Wagner's expanded
definition of dance), could create coherent meaning became
a vexing problem for him. For the doctrine he had formulated with such uncompromising severity in *Opera and
Drama* was hardly to be reconciled with Schopenhauer's
metaphysics of music, which exerted such a strong attrac-
tion over him—hardly surprisingly at the time of the genesis
of *Tristan*.

(The practice of applying the term "absolute" music only
to instrumental music without program or verbal text hin-
ders a formulation of the problem in its historical context,
conditioned by the assumptions of nineteenth-century aesthetics. Wagner's primary concern in his campaign against
"absolute" music was the question of the function and significance of music in musical drama and vocal music as a
whole: whether music was the "founding" and "motivat-
ing" element or whether it was "founded" in and "motivated" by other elements. Acknowledgment of the aesthetic
right of "pure instrumental music" to exist was then merely
a consequence of being persuaded that music could be meaningful of itself—without an extra-musical "formal motive."
Since Wagner altered his aesthetic interpretation of musical
drama, he was able in the end to accept Bruckner and even,
at the end of his life, to toy with the idea of writing symphonies himself. The idea of "absolute" music means that,
possessing meaning and coherence in its own right, music
can be the founding element aesthetically—but not genetically—when it is vocal music, as well as stand on its own
feet when it is purely instrumental.)

In Wagner's 1870 essay on Beethoven his acknowledgment of Schopenhauer, which is the form in which he expresses the change in his attitude towards his own work
(Wagner never absorbed anything from outside unless he had
an inner need and use for it), comes close to quotation.

Music does not represent the ideas contained in the phenomena
of the world; it is itself an idea, a comprehensive idea, of the

world. Of itself music includes drama entirely within itself, since drama in turn expresses the only idea of the world which is commensurate with music. . . . Just as drama does not depict human characters but enables them to present themselves directly, so a piece of music, in its motives, gives us the character of all the phenomena of the world according to their innermost essence. The movement, formation and alteration of these motives, by analogy, are not only related solely to the drama: but the drama, representing the idea, can in truth be understood with perfect clarity only through the medium of those musical motives and in the way they move, form, and alter.[50]

Music, which *is* an idea, is the origin of drama, which *represents* an idea. In 1872, in his essay *On the Term "Music Drama,"* Wagner spoke of his dramas as "deeds of music which have become visible."[51] Music is the "essence" *(Wesen)*, to which drama stands in the relationship of "material appearance" *(sinnliches Scheinen)*, in Hegelian terminology.

There are no more references to "absolute" music; Wagner has dropped the term altogether—probably to avoid using it with a positive, instead of negative, emphasis and so making the disjunction in his aesthetic theory more obvious than it was already. But there is no denying that the concept designated by the term is implicitly present as one of the central categories in Wagner's later writings on aesthetics. The turning point—and apparently his last use of the term—is marked by the open letter *On Franz Liszt's Symphonic Poems* (1857), in which the change in Wagner's ideas, though unacknowledged, reveals itself in the ambiguity of his formulations. At first Wagner appears to be still loyal to the thesis he expounded in *Opera and Drama*, that music needs an extra-musical "formal motive" (a non-musical reason for existing at all) if it is to make sense and express anything.

Nothing is less absolute than music *(nota bene:* where its appearance in life is concerned), and those who champion the cause of an absolute music

50. Ibid., 9:105f.   51. Ibid., 9:306.

—the expression Wagner had invented in his reforming essays of the early 1850s had in the meantime been adopted by Hanslick, in 1854, and used in an apologetic sense[52]—

> evidently do not know what they mean; to confound them it would be enough to ask them to show us a piece of music without the form which it took from physical movement or words (according to the causal nexus).[53]

But the parentheses betray Wagner's philosophical embarrassment. It is uncertain whether by "causal nexus" he means only the historical provenance of "pure instrumental music" out of dance music (as such fulfilling a function) and vocal music (which it imitated) or whether he also means the dependence of a dramatic score on the prescribed text and scenario; it is of no great importance to decide, since both meanings are open to the objection that the genesis of a musical form cannot be automatically equated with its aesthetic validity. The banal fact that text and scenario precede music (the few exceptions, such as in the case of *Tristan*, do not affect the general rule) does not prevent the text and the stage action from appearing as a translation and simile of the music (as Nietzsche put it) when the work is completed. The first parenthesis—"(*nota bene:* where [music's] appearance in life is concerned)"—obviously refers to the distinction between genesis and significance, between empirical, biographical facts and metaphysical, aesthetic truth. Metaphysically, the music is the "origin" of the drama; empirically, in compositional practice, it is "conditioned" by the drama.

> On this we are agreed and admit that divine music in this human world had to be given a conjunctive, indeed—as we have seen—a conditioning element to make its appearance possible.[54]

52. Hanslick, *Vom Musikalisch-Schönen*, p. 20.
53. Wagner, *Gesammelte Schriften*, 5:191.
54. Ibid., 5:192 (*Über Franz Liszts symphonische Dichtungen*).

"Conditionality" is forced upon a composer who needs to meet some form of opposition in order to be creative, and "unconditionality" on a listener who recognizes aesthetic contemplation, as described by Schopenhauer, as a vehicle of metaphysical insight.

5

The idea of an "absolute," "unconditional" music, needing no extra-musical "formal motive" to be meaningful, is one of the central aesthetic tenets of a century in which art music (not the vast majority of the music that was written, which remained in the shadows) rose to aesthetic "autonomy," that is, no longer had a manifest function to fulfill, but was intended to be listened to for its own sake. Of course "autonomous" music often had an "ideological" or prestige function imposed upon it, but that does not alter the fact that there is a palpable distinction in principle between "functional" and "autonomous" music.

The word "absolute" is an equivocal one, signifying the absolving of music from the obligation to fulfill extra-musical functions and subject itself to texts and programs, as well as suggesting an affinity to the metaphysical category of the "absolute," but this is by no means a terminological weakness which ought to be eliminated by stricter definition. Rather it is an exact verbal equivalent of the aesthetic idea the term seeks to express: the idea that music is given metaphysical significance by the very fact that as an "autonomous" art it forms "a separate world of its own";[55] the "essence" that lies beyond the "appearance" reveals itself, according to Schopenhauer and Nietzsche, to the listener who forgets self (escapes from "individuation") and immerses himself in music, in the immanent dynamic and logic of the sound. It is "absolute" music, music which is independent of a text or of the need to illustrate one, which

55. L. Tieck, "Die Töne," in W. H. Wackenroder, *Werke und Briefe* (Heidelberg, 1967), p. 245.

reveals or intimates the "spirit realm," E. T. A. Hoffmann's "Djinnistan": music, that is, which either exists in its own right without text, scenario, or program, or possesses an aesthetic superiority beside which the text that is associated with it fades to a mere simile of the sounding "revelation from another world."[56]

The claim that the metaphysics of "absolute" music— not the emotional theory of aesthetics inherited from the eighteenth century, and not Wagner's "exoteric" theory of extra-musical "formal motives"—is the true musical aesthetic of the nineteenth century, the age of musical "autonomy," from Friedrich Schlegel, E. T. A. Hoffmann, and Schopenhauer to Hanslick, Wagner, and Nietzsche, emerges from the construction of an "ideal type" in the Weberian sense,[57] not a simple summary of what is to be found in the sources. Strictly speaking, it is only Schlegel, Hoffmann, and later Nietzsche who expound a theory of "absolute" music that ventures without qualification on the metaphysical, or (to invert the formulation) a metaphysics of which "absolute" music is an organon—music, that is, which is not founded on emotions, but of which the emotions can be regarded as similes, as secondary reflections. Schopenhauer melded the metaphysics of music with the emotional theory of aesthetics (though in an abstract form), Hanslick was opposed to metaphysics (though not as independent of Hegel as he claimed to be), and Wagner modified the metaphysics of music (of "absolute" music, though he did not call it by that name) with an empirical theory of "conditional" music.

The construction of "ideal types" is not only legitimate but inevitable if the writing of history—the history of music no less than that of politics—is not to stifle beneath the rubble of facts. There is moreover the circumstance that Nietzsche drew critical conclusions from the aesthetic theories of Schopenhauer, Hanslick, and Wagner which pin-

56. Wagner, *Gesammelte Schriften*, 9:96 (*Beethoven*).
57. M. Weber, *Gesammelte Aufsätze zur Wissenschaftslehre*, 3d ed. (Tübingen, 1968), pp. 190ff.

point the spot where the originally separate or even contradictory theories converge to create a metaphysics of "absolute" music. The historical significance of the fragment
"On Music and Words" is that Nietzsche, in an unconscious
referral back to romanticism, formulated a comprehensive
concept of "absolute" music which reveals the latent unity
of musical aesthetics in the nineteenth century.

Issues in Composition

❦

1. The musical idea

Richard Strauss once observed that the melodic ideas which provide the substance of a composition seldom consist of more than two to four bars; the remainder is elaboration, working-out, compositional technique.[1] The aesthetic crux that he touched on here is one which occupied the Greeks and has not lost its teasing character with age: the perennial question of the priority of reflection or inspiration, *ars* or *ingenium*, technique or genius. The aesthetic discussion has to be located in a historical context, however, if it is not to remain on a plane of abstract speculation. Certainly the limited dimensions of the kind of thematic inspiration to which Strauss referred are characteristic not so much of all musical creativity at all times as of composition in the latter part of the nineteenth century. It is no exaggeration to say that the difficulties faced by composers after Beethoven were due in no small part to the brevity of their musical ideas: these difficulties were shared by Wagner, Liszt, Bruckner, and even Brahms, although their solutions differed. Nietzsche's axiom that it was necessary to close one's

1. R. Strauss, "Vom melodischen Einfall," in *Betrachtungen und Erinnerungen*, 2d ed. (Zurich, 1957), p. 165.

eyes to Wagner the "al fresco painter" if one was to discover the true Wagner—"our greatest musical miniaturist"[2]— employs a metaphor to describe something that could be expressed as the contradiction between the brevity of the musical ideas and the monumentality of the formal designs.

It could be argued that brevity of musical ideas was à characteristic not of the later nineteenth century alone but of Beethoven himself, at least in the symphonies, but this was not the case; the *Eroica* and the Fifth Symphony may spring to mind, but Wagner's formal problems are different in kind from Beethoven's. The eight-note theme—or "motto"—of the first movement of the *Eroica* is determined by the overall design and not vice versa: the form is not built up out of the theme. The motto is not so much stated or expounded and then developed as brought forth by the symphonic process in which it has a function to fulfill, and the musical "idea" is the symphonic process itself, not the theme. The opening of the Fifth Symphony is analogous: as Heinrich Schenker demonstrated,[3] the belief that the first four notes constitute the thematic substance of the movement is, however popular, mistaken. The melodic idea is not what is contained in the first two bars, repeated sequentially in the third and fourth (more than that would have to be taken into account, if one wished to define the "idea" in the Beethovenian sense); it is the whole of bars 1–4, the twofold descending third (G–E♭ and F–D) which in the subsidiary theme becomes a descending fifth, also repeated (B♭–E♭ and F–B♭). (The structural similarity of the thematic openings indicates that the sequential working belongs to the thematic idea and not to the elaboration.) But the error as to the structure of the theme—one shared by even Wagner himself[4]—is historically revealing. What to Beethoven was a part, a component, was understood later in the nineteenth century to be an independent, self-sufficient musical idea,

2. F. Nietzsche, *Der Fall Wagner*, in *Werke*, 2:918.
3. H. Schenker, *Beethoven: V. Symphonie* (Vienna, n.d.), pp. 3ff.
4. Wagner, *Gesammelte Schriften*, 8:282 (*Über das Dirigieren*).

because the composers of the day looked for and found in Beethoven what they themselves practised. The original melodic unit represented by bars 1–4 was broken up and described as model and sequential repetition, so that it conformed to the pattern which was fundamental to the musical syntax of thematic openings written by Wagner and Liszt, whereas in the early nineteenth century sequence was a technique employed in elaboration and development, never in exposition. Of course Beethoven's theme can be described, in terms of its technical elements, as a model and sequential repetition, but the important distinction is whether the theme is understood primarily as a unit, whose sequential structure is a secondary factor, or whether, erroneously, the first four notes are treated as an idea complete in itself, which is then elaborated sequentially. In Beethoven formal ideas and melodic detail come into being simultaneously: the single motive is relative to the whole. By contrast, in the later nineteenth century the melodic idea acted as a motive in the literal sense of the word, setting the music in motion, and provided the substance of a development in which the theme itself was elaborated. Musical form now presented itself primarily (though by no means exclusively) as a consequence drawn from thematic ideas, not as a system of formal relations.

At least one reason for the extreme concision of the musical idea and for the consequent need to distinguish between the initial idea and its elaboration is to be found in the social and intellectual preconceptions of the time. The concept of originality which grew up in the later eighteenth century established itself in the nineteenth as an unquestioned aesthetic doctrine, whereas the idea of *ars inveniendi*, the theory of musical invention which was taken for granted in the seventeenth century and earlier in the eighteenth, was condemned in the nineteenth as if it were a blasphemy against the cult of genius.

Until the end of the eighteenth century a musical idea could be a platitude, something quite commonplace, with-

out attracting the charge of being meaningless; convention—recognizable dependence on precedent—was still
regarded as aesthetically legitimate. That is not to say that
no one could distinguish between an individual and unusual idea and a well-worn cliché, but the quality of an entire movement was not considered to depend entirely on the
originality of the idea expounded at its start.

The thematic technique of classical composers around
1800 represents a transitional stage, achieving a balance, at
once felicitous and precarious, between opposing aesthetic
principles. The originality for which Haydn and Beethoven
undoubtedly strove and the amount of formal convention
which was still acceptable complemented each other without contradiction, since the dichotomy—which is often apparent aesthetically—was not the decisive structural factor.
As yet the single idea was still understood primarily as a
corollary of the whole, and not as the essential sustaining
substance, whose individuality or conventionality determined the overall form and was the only grounds on which
its quality might be judged. Both Wagner and Schoenberg
complain about the mere padding to be found in Mozart's
music, even in some of his principal themes, but this is almost unavoidable when the musical form is made up of
corresponding, well-balanced parts which of themselves delineate the whole movement. Such form resembles the metrical pattern adopted in a poem, by contrast with the musical "prose" which results when melodic ideas are expressed plainly without periphrasis. In the first movement
of Mozart's C major Symphony K.551, the continuation of
the first thematic period—a tutti described by Hans Georg
Nägeli as "shallow" and "trivial"[5]—can be justified by its
function, which is to provide a counterbalance to the opening of the movement, even if it is indefensible in terms of
melodic or harmonic invention, of which it has none.
Classical form could survive banality in some (not all) of its

5. H. G. Nägeli, *Vorlesungen über Musik mit Berücksichtigung der Di-
lettanten* (Stuttgart, 1826), pp. 164f.

parts: the banal did not become intolerable until the idea of
a balance of parts distinguished by their functions was replaced by the principle of developing ideas, the concept of
musical form as something which presented the history of a
musical theme.

During the course of the nineteenth century, for socio-
historical reasons among others, it became virtually obligatory for themes, or their initial ideas, to be original, because
form itself fell into a state of one-sided dependence on the
musical idea. Schematic forms, of the kind predominating in
short character pieces for piano, were sustained exclusively
by the quality of the initial idea, the individual character of
which compensated for the conventionality of the overall
outline. (The fact that the differentiated formulation and
development of ideas can be accommodated in conventional
ABA formal patterns in the piano music of Schumann or
Brahms would be an almost irreconcilable contradiction,
were it not that the formal outline serves no other purpose
than to present and arrange the musical "content.") Individualized form is the polar opposite of schematic form (the
tendency to create it can be observed in some of Liszt's symphonic poems); it represents the consequential unfurling of
the initial musical idea (which, for its part, is determined
programmatically), and its success in formulating and pre-
senting the musical content can be measured by how well
it conceals the fact that it is doing so.[6]

In a form in which every part or detail is supposed to be an
original idea or the consequence of an original idea, conventional material is bound to be regarded as superfluous padding, and a work in which platitudes are conspicuous will be
condemned aesthetically as derivative hackwork. No phrase
in a theme or its continuation should be empty of meaning,
the mere formulaic expansion of the essential musical idea
to a regular verse-like period (symmetry and rounding-off,
the essential premises of a form conceived of as a "poetic"

6. Wagner, *Gesammelte Schriften*, 5:187f (*Über Franz Liszts symphonische Dichtungen*).

metrical pattern on a large scale, are almost unimaginable without conventional components and interpolations). By contrast, when musical ideas are wholly original, significant at every instant and expressed without padding, as Richard Strauss said, they are apt to be extremely short. Leitmotivs as long as the Siegfried motive are the exception in Wagner, not the rule; the Sword and Spear motives are representative of the norm.

The type of motive represented by the Curse motive in *Der Ring des Nibelungen* and the Day motive in *Tristan und Isolde*, a type which was regarded in the later nineteenth century as the paradigm of a musical idea in the emphatic sense of the word, is not subject to the laws governing the distinction between "open" and "closed" syntactic structures; the usual categories do not apply to it. On the one hand these motives come to an end without a perfect or imperfect cadence; harmonically undetermined, they suggest that more is to follow. On the other hand their rhythmic outlines are so clear-cut that continuation is unnecessary as a means of giving them syntactic sense or identity. Thus the motive is neither a complete period in itself, nor will it tolerate the construction of a consequent clause to make it up to a period. The idea that the Yearning motive in *Tristan* needs a motivically analogous and harmonically complementary clause to "complete" it is inexpressibly trivial; the only suitable means of continuing the motive is sequential repetition, which leads it into tonally remote regions.

2. Real sequence and developing variation

The technique of real, "literal" sequence, which effects an interruption or an actual change of the initial key, acquires in Wagner and Liszt—and Liszt's symphonic poems seem to have had some influence on Wagner[7]—a formal significance which is different in principle from the "same" procedure as used by Haydn or Beethoven. In classical symphonic or

7. C. Dahlhaus, *Wagners Konzeption des musikalischen Dramas* (Regensburg, 1971), pp. 111ff.

sonata movements, "real" (or modulatory, but not tonal) sequence was used primarily as a developmental technique, one part in the process of musical working-out, which had invariably been preceded by an exposition section where the themes had been stated in a form both tonally and syntactically complete. (The fact that sequential models are drawn into expansive modulatory processes in the course of a development section is closely connected with their melodic formation out of fragments of a theme or of several themes: the dissolution of the harmonic and tonal outlines is felt to be the correlative of melodic and syntactical dissolution. The unrest of the modulation, like the thematic instability, corresponds to the transitional stage reached in the formal process.)

In Wagner and Liszt, on the other hand (and sometimes in Bruckner too, e.g. the beginning of the Sixth Symphony), real sequence is an expository procedure, a means of elaborating a musical idea which in itself—like the Yearning motive in *Tristan*—needs no continuation and would not tolerate conventional "rounding-off" in a closed period. In Liszt's symphonic poem *Hamlet*, the principal section of which is no less than 159 bars long, the principal theme (bar 105) is the goal and the outcome of an extended development which relies essentially on acceleration of tempo and transformation of themes. The individual musical ideas are spread out in sequences, either real or modulatory, according to a tonal pattern which seems at times excessively schematic. (In bars 9ff. the model, which is repeated, modulates from C minor to A♭ minor, and the sequence modulates from E♭ minor to B minor; the principal theme is stated complete in B minor and D minor, and fragments are then transposed to A♭ minor, E minor and D♭ major.) It might be thought that the sequential structure is determined and justified at the start by the introductory character of the parts, and in the main theme by the merging of exposition and development (the transposition of the theme from B minor to D minor both prepares and starts the evolution).

The form is unusual: an expansive introduction eventually arrives at a principal theme which, after a brief moment of actual "exposition" in the sonata-form sense, moves on into development. Yet it seems as though the sequential structure is not a product of the unusual form but, on the contrary, the form is a consequence of the sequential structure, which is itself motivated by the brevity of the musical ideas. This lends more support to the theory that conceptions of musical form are based, in each era, on the characteristic types of thematic material, of melodic invention, than to the opposing notion, that thematic types are produced by formal ideas.

It would be wrong to dismiss the change in the function of modulatory sequence from a developmental technique to an expositional technique as an event of merely peripheral significance in the history of composition. Changes in the functions of musical techniques are historically of no less (even if less apparent) importance than the substantial, material developments—such as the growing prominence of chromaticism and the exploration of remoter tonal regions—which are normally regarded as the signs of musical progress in the nineteenth century. If the importance of a change is measured in terms of its influence on musical form, understood as the sum of the associations between all the elements in a composition, it is by no means possible to assert *a priori* that the invasion of expositional processes by modulatory sequence had a less profound effect than the chromaticization of harmony.

In Wagner and Liszt the change in the function of real, modulatory sequence is the formal outcome of the kind of thematic writing epitomized by the leitmotiv, which does not permit the formation of regular periods or submit to the regulations of large-scale metrical patterns. Brahms, faced like them with the difficulties caused by the concision of the basic thematic substance under the pressure of the all-pervading insistence on originality, sought a different solution in the procedure that Schoenberg was to call "developing variation." The latent unity of the music of the age is demonstrated by the fact that essentially the same problem faced Wagner, Liszt *and* Brahms; it is not reflected in stylistic unity or uniformity, however, since individual stylistic traits, which develop in the course of working out solutions, are not contingent on separate initial problems. The difference between these composers is discovered in the methods which they employed to resolve or annul the discrepancy between the narrow dimensions of thematic ideas and the tendency towards large, expansive, monumental forms: a tendency that Brahms the symphonist—an aspiring symphonist even in the structure of his chamber music—shared with Wagner the composer of music dramas. Real (modulatory) sequence and developing variation are alternatives to each other in practical musical terms, without mutually excluding each other in principle. As expositional procedures they can be said to represent the practices of what Franz Brendel in 1859 dubbed the "New German" school of composition on the one hand and the "conservatives" on the other (although, as the progressive consequences that Schoenberg drew from Brahms's techniques demonstrate, the latter were by no means as backward-looking as may have appeared in 1870 or 1880).

In his own way Brahms was as much a "musical miniaturist" as Wagner and Liszt, nurturing the same ambitions to use large, all-embracing, "Beethovenian" forms. The serenades and the First Piano Concerto are milestones on his way towards the symphony, the monumental demands of which he did not feel himself ready to meet for another two decades. Beginning with thematic substance that was reduced—one might almost say shrunk—to the utmost, he had to evolve a technique of formal elaboration which would carry over wide spans without subsiding into vacuous academic discursiveness.

The use Brahms made of developing variation as an expositional procedure (that is, in a formal function similar to that of modulatory sequence in Wagner and Liszt) is exemplified in the first movement of the G minor Piano Quartet op. 25. The material of the principal section (bars 1–27) derives from two motives of the utmost brevity and, in themselves, no great significance: the first consists of four notes, the second of two. The first part of the theme is based on the motivic shape which appears as D–B♭–F♯–G in bar 1, transposed in bar 5, and freely inverted, either as in bars 2–3 and 6–8, or with the two middle notes played simultaneously (bar 4: F♯–C♯–E–D):

The second part of the theme consists of nothing more than a descending second, which is repeated sequentially and imitatively (bars 11–13) and appears in all manner of rhythmic shapes: in half-notes (bars 11–13, 20) and dotted half-notes (bars 17–18), in eighth-notes (bars 13–15) and in quarters (bars 15–16). Compositional economy, the building of musical interest out of minimal capital, was taken to extremes by Brahms.

The process of developing variation bestows on both the basic motives and the material derived from them—insofar as it is recognizable as such—a meaning that they would not have in themselves, as isolated figures. The whole significance of the musical instant, unimportant in itself, is that it points the way forward to something greater. Even if it is agreed, however, that the musical meaning of the individual phrases is dependent on the relationship in which they stand to each other and to the initial idea, this is still not enough to characterize the material; as in the case, already mentioned, of the first tutti of Mozart's "Jupiter" Symphony, it is only the relationship to the opening period that gives the music its aesthetic justification. But in Mozart's case the musical form can be compared to architecture (and was, by Friedrich Schlegel), whereas in Brahms it is like the development or elaboration, both logical and rhetorical, of a process of thought. Mozart does not by any means despise using his initial ideas as a source of further thematic and motivic material, but doing so always serves a function. It is subordinated to the principle of balance which dominates and controls his forms of whatever order, from the subordinate clause to the overall outline of the whole: the motivic correspondence between a first-subject group and a transition, as much as the motivic contrast between a second-subject group and a closing section, is a procedure intended to balance corresponding parts. (The provision of links and analogies between a first subject and a transition is of lesser importance: it does not constitute a structural principle but is merely an expedient—for which others could be substituted—for demonstrating that the sections are complementary.) With Brahms, on the other hand, the elaboration of a thematic idea is the primary formal principle, on which depends the integration of the movement as a whole, preventing it from appearing as a mere pot-pourri. Musical form takes the shape of a discourse in sound in which motives develop out of earlier motives like ideas, each of which is a consequence of its predecessors.

The differences in the technical procedures adopted by Wagner and Liszt on the one hand and by Brahms on the other are of course, like the stances taken up by opposing parties in the musical life of the later nineteenth century as a whole, closely connected with the differences between the preferred genres—between music drama and chamber music; this has always been recognized. (Wagner's chamber compositions are mere parerga—curiosities with no real bearing on the central part of his oeuvre—and likewise it is no accident that Brahms never carried out his operatic plans.) Sequential writing on the scale and in the manner in

which it occurs in Wagner and Liszt, if found in the exposition of a piece of chamber music, would strike the listener
as unwelcome tonal discursiveness and pompous rhetoric.
Developing variation, for its part, would fall flat in music
drama: it would be nothing but a pedantic self-indulgence by
the composer, it would not penetrate the listener's awareness in performance, and aesthetically—in any bearing it
might have on the realization of the drama—it would still
be ineffectual even for someone reading the score who was
able to see the latent associations. Wagner's technique of
motivic transformation, such as the growth of the Valhalla
motive out of the Ring motive during the transition between
the first and second scenes of *Das Rheingold*, is a procedure
that is an exception rather than the rule in music drama. It is
imposed on the music by the dramatic program and is not at
all the same thing as the unobtrusive, yet completely con-
vincing, musical logic of the developing variation in
Brahms's G minor Piano Quartet.

The symphony can be said to occupy a middle ground,
stylistically, between the large canvas of music drama and
the intimate discourse of chamber music, and in it the divergent techniques characteristic of those two contrasting
genres in their most typical manifestations tend to overlap
and blend. It has always been recognized that Brahms's
symphonic writing is rooted in the premises of chamber
music, but there has never been any question of regarding it
simply as chamber music in disguise: rather it is a matter of
transformation. The process undergone by the "motto" of
the first movement of the Third Symphony is a paradigm of
developing variation when transferred from chamber music
to the monumental dimensions of the symphony. The motive expounded in the introduction, which is the fundamental musical idea of the movement, though it does not function as the principal subject, constantly recurs in changing
harmonizations wherever there is what could be called a
"hinge" in the form. The variation of the harmony is not

coloristic in intention, but corresponds functionally to the various changes in the situation and significance of the motto (establishing the basic key at the beginning; providing the bass line in a harmonically ambiguous antecedent clause; preparing the second subject by modulation); it can therefore be described as a "developing" variation—one, that is, which affects the formal progress, and not simply one which provides transient coloring. On the other hand, the motivic shape of the motto is always recognizable, so that it can continue to fulfill the role of establishing connections over the wide span of a symphony.

If Brahms was attempting in his Third Symphony to combine the pregnant significance of the leitmotiv, which strictly speaking cannot develop, with the principle of developing variation, Bruckner at the beginning of his Sixth Symphony introduces the Lisztian practice of using modulatory sequences in thematic exposition. This works in a symphonic poem like *Hamlet*, because there the distinction between exposition and development is ultimately unimportant, but the basic form of a symphonic movement still rests on the traditional distinction. The "dynamism" of incessantly modulating sequences contradicts the essentially "thematic" importance of the exposition, which should create the background against which development can take place. But if such conflict sometimes occurs in the symphony, in the middle ground between the poles of chamber music and music drama, and puts the form at risk, it confirms rather than refutes the correlation between a musical genre and its "ideal type" of expositional technique.

3. "Musical prose" and "endless melody"

The shrinking of thematic ideas created problems for composers all the greater because it coincided with the later nineteenth century's obsession with ever larger forms. This was a tendency for which it is hard to find inherent historical musical reasons, so an explanation must be sought in social and cultural history. (That is not to say that interpretation on socio-historical lines should, as a matter of principle, take over where the history of compositional procedures breaks off: in one sense each offers an alternative to the other, but there is also a stage at which one approach is transformed into the other.) The fact that thematic material was reduced during the course of the nineteenth century from the period to the motive was the result, as has been said, of the principle that a musical idea, to be worthy of the name, had to be original and meaningful throughout; a platitude lost the aesthetic right to exist that it was still allowed to enjoy as a component in a larger figure in Beethoven (in spite of the dominance of the doctrine of originality). Particles that lacked any special melodic character or content, but met a functional need insofar as they rounded off a musical idea to bring a phrase or a period to a formal conclusion, could no longer be tolerated. Such aesthetic rigor was linked with the emphasis that the age of romanticism, with its cult of genius, laid on inspiration, but it threatened to undermine traditional musical syntax and the regular periodic structure which provided the framework of musical form—that is, of form conceived of as a large-scale metrical pattern. "Quadratic compositional construction," as Wagner scornfully called it—in a failure to appreciate the architectural nature of a formal principle based on the idea of balance, a principle which Alfred Lorenz wrongly asserted to be the "secret" of Wagnerian form—is scarcely imaginable without some melodic filling-out.

In an essay with the provocative title "Brahms the Progressive," Arnold Schoenberg, whose initiation of the atonal techniques of the New Music in 1908 signified not only a break with the past but also, and simultaneously, one of the ultimate consequences of the compositional trends of the nineteenth century, spoke of "musical prose."[8] The term

8. A. Schoenberg, *Style and Idea* (New York, 1950), p. 72 [2d ed., 1976, p. 415]; cf. also Dahlhaus, "Musikalische Prosa," *Neue Zeitschrift für Musik*, vol. 125 (1964): 176 ff.

should make it plain that the rhythmic and metrical irregularity of which the New Music was accused—and which
was as great a hindrance to its acceptance as atonal harmony[9]—was not a sign of wanton destructiveness but the
necessary outcome when composers undertook to express a
musical idea directly, without circumlocution or ornament.
(Schoenberg shared Adolf Loos's hostility towards ornamentation.) Periodic structure, the musical equivalent of "verse"
form, is open to the charge of creating opportunities for
empty rhetoric and interpolations which express little or
nothing. Melody, as popularly conceived, is characterized
above all by rhythmic regularity, by the use of symmetry
and repetition: this was a "formula," in opposition to which
Schoenberg set up the musical "idea," which is expressed
"like prose" (*prosaisch*). "This is what musical prose should
be—a direct and straightforward presentation of ideas,
without any patchwork, without mere padding and empty
repetitions."[10] The traditions of which Schoenberg was the
continuer and which he took to their ultimate consequences
were those of the nineteenth century; this is his justification
for applying to earlier works the categories that doubtless
originated in his own compositional experiences although
he developed them in analysing Brahms and Mozart. These
categories represent an extreme statement of their case and
therefore should not always be taken literally, but some of
the essential facts and associations in nineteenth-century
music cannot be revealed or explained by any other means.

The rejection of what were felt to be empty melodic formulas and the consequent tendency towards rhythmic and
metric irregularity (that is, the recoil from both symmetrical
periods and the filling-out necessary if symmetry was to be
achieved) are closely connected with the conception of
melody for which, in the essay *Music of the Future*, Wagner
invented the term "endless melody."[11] The concept's sub-

9. A. Berg, "Warum ist Schönbergs Musik so schwer verständlich," in
W. Reich, *Alban Berg* (Vienna, 1937), pp. 142ff.

10. Schoenberg, *Style and Idea*, p. 72 [p. 415].

11. Wagner, *Gesammelte Schriften*, 7:130.

sequent terminological career obviously owes less to a precise understanding of its original meaning than to the vague associations that have attached themselves to it.[12] Bemused by the word "endless," people have forgotten to enquire what Wagner understood by "melody."

In Wagner's vocabulary "melody" is primarily an aesthetic category, not a technical compositional one: what is musically eloquent and meaningful is "melodic" in this positive sense, what is formulaic and inexpressive is "unmelodic." Schoenberg's reputedly "unmelodic" musical language is consistently "melodic" by Wagner's criteria. A melody is "narrow" (to use the terminology of *Music of the Future* again) if the truly melodic is forever breaking off, as in Italian opera, to be replaced by "unmelodic" filling-out. In Wagner's historico-aesthetic scheme of things, Italian opera, as exemplified by Rossini, is at the opposite pole to the symphonic writing of Beethoven. (In a context where Italian opera is not the subject under discussion it is permissible to ignore the stylistic dualism of the nineteenth century, that is, to overlook the fact that it makes no sense historically to judge the tradition of Rossini by the criteria of the Beethovenian tradition, or vice versa.) Wagner was convinced that any listener whose musical sensibilities had not been blunted by too much "narrow" operatic melody of the kind that amateur enthusiasts took for the quintessence of melody was bound to "acknowledge that every note in the harmony, yea, every pause in the rhythm [in a symphony by Beethoven] has melodic significance."[13] The principle of expression, of eloquence *(das redende Prinzip)* is what determines Wagner's concept of melody.[14] He once demonstrated this concept to Felix Draeseke by singing as much as he could of the first movement of the *Eroica* before he ran out

12. F. Reckow, "Unendliche Melodie," in *Handwörterbuch der musikalischen Terminologie* (Wiesbaden, 1973).
13. Wagner, *Gesammelte Schriften*, 7:127 *(Zukunftsmusik)*.
14. A. Schering, "Carl Philipp Emanuel Bach und das 'redende Prinzip' in der Musik," in *Vom musikalischen Kunstwerk*, 2d ed. (Leipzig, 1951), pp. 213ff.

of breath, and judged by that criterion the movement, since not a note of it is superfluous or inexpressive, is indeed "nothing other than a single, perfectly coherent melody."[15]

The single, uninterrupted melody that Wagner found embodied in Beethoven's symphonies is a forerunner, even the prototype, of the "endless melody" that he himself realized in music drama. (The essential difference between Beethoven's works and his own, as Wagner saw it, lies in the transition from the indeterminate "meaning" of the melody in Beethoven to the meaning it derives from the drama in Wagner.) Thus the primary meaning of the term "endless melody," which is often misused and should by no means be treated exclusively as a technical expression, is not that the parts of a work flow into each other without caesuras but that every note has meaning, that the melody is language and not empty sound. The technical characteristic, the absence of formal cadences, is merely a consequence of the aesthetic factor: cadences are regarded as formulas, syntactic but not semantic components—in short, they express nothing and are therefore to be avoided or concealed.

There would seem to be no way of accommodating the idea of "endless melody" to the precarious concision that we have seen to be characteristic of melodic ideas in the music of the later nineteenth century, but if we ignore terminological externals, we can recognize that the former is the correlative of the latter. Their all-important common premise is a rejection of ornament and filling-out. In an age in which musical form had ceased to be regarded primarily as a matter of large-scale metrical patterns, the formal function carried out previously by ornamentation and filling-out was almost forgotten.

If, in the words of Wagner's dictum, "an endless melody" has to be "perfectly coherent," it means that the individual musical events and shapes ought to proceed out of each other, instead of being arrayed side by side, linked by mean-

15. Wagner, *Gesammelte Schriften*, 7:127 (*Zukunftsmusik*).

ingless padding and with no inner relationships. Brahms, sharing Wagner's concern to "justify" musical processes, would certainly have endorsed his postulate. Freedom from inconsequentiality can either be a matter of formal logic, as in Brahms's chamber music, or, as in Wagner's music dramas, it can obey a logic transmitted primarily (though not solely) by "content." (The invention of a polarity between "formalism" on the one hand and "the aesthetic theory of content" on the other was a typical piece of nine-teenth-century silliness and created a spurious dogmatic conflict between parties, both of which shared a concern with the whole nature of music. The dialectics of form and content and the historical shifts in the definitions of the two terms mean that the conflict could at best be a matter of altering the emphasis on one or the other. Nevertheless, the polarity has its uses in furnishing a provisional means of identifying tendencies in formal creative processes which are bound up with differences between genres.)

An inherent postulate of the idea of "endless melody" is that throughout the course of a piece of music each instant will possess a "significance" equal to that of every other instant. This resulted in the shrinking of the thematic period—part of which was necessarily formulaic in com-position—to the short, as it were "prose-like," shape of the individual musical idea. And the apparently mutually con-tradictory factors, brevity and endlessness, can be recon-ciled—on the basis of their common aesthetic premise—so long as the composer succeeds in mediating between the individual parts and the whole, between the original idea and the wide span of his form. But in the later nineteenth century opinions about the methods of mediation—the structural principles—adopted by composers were colored by aesthetic prejudices and partiality, which blinded the adherents of both sides to the fact that the composers' prob-lems were fundamentally the same. The primarily "formal" elaboration of musical ideas in Brahms was regarded by those Wagnerians hostile to him not as a process in which one could acknowledge the "melodic significance" of every note but as inexpressive musical academicism. Similarly, the "formalists" in the anti-Wagner camp would not acknowledge that the role played by "content" in linking a series of leitmotivs constituted melodic continuity. With their restricted concept of music as something to which "drama" or a "program" could only be an external, nonmusical addition, they regarded the concatenation of motives which sometimes diverged abruptly from each other as mere cobbling.

But if the historian keeps aloof from the partisan squabbles of the later nineteenth century and, in obedience to the maxim that every musical phenomenon must be interpreted in the light of its own premises, recognizes that formal development in Brahms is the development of ideas (not the mechanical spinning of formulas) and, conversely, that the developments in Wagner which are transmitted by content are developing ideas (and not mere cobbling), he will perceive that the compositional issue that lies beyond the aesthetic, stylistic and formal cruxes is the same. Wagner and Liszt, no less than Brahms, conceived of music as discourse in sound, in which every detail should be an original idea (or the outcome of one) and the whole a logically constructed chain, every link justified by what has preceded it.

As he wrote with polemical emphasis in *Nietzsche contra Wagner*, Nietzsche saw "endless melody" as something which threatened to dissolve rhythm, by which he understood the perceptible ordering of musical motion, not merely durational structure. While earlier music walked or danced the new music tried to "float" or "hover." " 'Endless melody' sets out to disrupt all regularity of duration and accent, and in doing so it makes mock of them."[16]

Musical verse-form, the regular period composed symmetrically of antecedent and consequent clauses, was dissolved in Wagner's music dramas from *Das Rheingold* on, if

16. Nietzsche, *Werke*, 2:1043.

not into prose then into a kind of *vers libre* (the upsurge of which in French poetry cannot be wholly unconnected with the Symbolists' enthusiasm for Wagner). The decline of traditional musical syntax did endanger that classical or classico-romantic concept of musical form to which periodic structure—the relation of "proposition" *(Aufstellung)* and "response" *(Beantwortung)*, to use Hugo Riemann's terms—was fundamental. The balance of complementary parts—from the relationship between upbeats and downbeats to the answering of an antecedent clause by a consequent, from the relationship between exposition and development within one subject group to the contrasts between subject groups as a whole—was the fundamental principle of musical form in the eighteenth and early nineteenth centuries. The transition to "logical" form, form determined by the development of musical ideas, is half accomplished in Beethoven; he did not, however, jettison architectural form altogether but held the divergent principles poised in a precarious balance. Even in Wagner's *Lohengrin*, which the composer was terminologically and historically quite correct to call a "romantic opera" and not a music drama, the music consists for long stretches at a time of periods, the regularity of which ensures formal coherence.[17]

With the dissolution of regular periodic structure, music drama from *Das Rheingold* onwards used in its place a much more fully developed leitmotivic technique. Leitmotivs had already been used in *Lohengrin* to emphasize and comment musically on isolated elements in the drama, but now they were spread over entire works in a dense network of motivic relationships: that is, the technique assumed the function of creating the musical form. It took a long time for anyone to acknowledge that musical form can be a polythematic network, a "web" or "woven fabric" *(Gewebe)* as Wagner called it himself, instead of having to be either architectural or the extended elaboration of a few thematic ideas. For didactic

17. Dahlhaus, *Wagners Konzeption des musikalischen Dramas*, pp. 50ff.

reasons, theorists of form tended always to favor simpler kinds of schematicism, and even in the 1920s Alfred Lorenz,[18] intending to refute the incessantly repeated charge that Wagner's music was amorphous, expounded what he regarded as the "architectural" principles underlying Wagner's form: for the most part these "principles" are figments of Lorenz's own imagination, conjured up in apologetic zeal.[19] There is as much aesthetic virtue in "reticulation" as in "grouping" and "elaboration" as means of creating musical form.

Thus leitmotivic technique plays a formal, structural role in Wagner equivalent to that of regular periodic structure in other music: the leitmotivs create the framework of the form instead of being interpolated, for dramaturgical reasons, into a structure that rests on other foundations. The replacement of the one formal principle by the other marks the transition from "romantic opera" to "music drama." (In a brief historiographic outline it is hardly necessary to say that an "ideal type" is here being constructed to describe a process which was far more complex in musico-historical reality; that is, it is not being claimed that leitmotivic technique plays no structural part at all in *Lohengrin*, nor that there is not one regular period in *Das Rheingold*. Groups of four and eight bars are not, of course, banished from the *Ring:* they are not even particularly infrequent, but they no longer provide the framework of the musical form as they did in *Lohengrin*.) Differentiation between regular and irregular syntax almost ceases to be of any formal importance or to exert any formal influence in the *Ring;* one could very well make an analogy with the "emancipation of dissonance" and speak of the emancipation of the metrically irregular phrase—which hereupon ceases to be irregular:

18. A. Lorenz, *Das Geheimnis der Form bei Richard Wagner*, 4 vols. (Berlin, 1924–33).

19. Dahlhaus, "Formprinzipien in Wagners 'Ring des Nibelungen'," in *Beiträge zur Geschichte der Oper*, ed. H. Becker (Regensburg, 1969), pp. 95ff.

whereas irregularity was previously an exception to a norm of regularity, a license, the purpose of which was understandable only by reference to that norm, emancipated irregularity exists in its own right. The "emancipation" does not mean that there is no longer any difference to be discerned between consonance and dissonance, or between "quadratic" and "non-quadratic" syntax, only that the difference is no longer an integral part of the musical structure: it exists, but it is no longer an element in the construction of the form. When there is continual alternation of "quadratic" and "non-quadratic" phrases—and the latter are not such as can be reduced to fit into quadratic structure—they do not add up to make periodic groups conforming to a large-scale metrical pattern; the effect of the "quadratic" phrases remains locked in the moment.

It is mistaken to suggest that the periodic framework of classical form was preserved intact by the "classicist" Brahms. Although his conservative tendencies can scarcely be denied, they do not mean that he revered the fundamentals of tradition while making modifications in some of the details, but rather that he radically rethought the traditional principles in the altered circumstances of the second half of the nineteenth century. Sonata form takes on a different meaning from the one it originally had when motivic development, the elaboration of thematic ideas, becomes the primary structural principle, in place of the pattern of key relationships and the construction of symmetrical groups. The form is "conserved," but by means which eventually made possible Schoenberg's development of atonal sonata form.

The principle of originality which was the reason for the brevity of musical ideas resulted, in the music of Brahms, in the technique of developing variation, used as a means not only of development but also of exposition. The opening of the B major Trio op. 8 is paradigmatic. The essential thematic idea is given in bars 1–2; bars 3–4 are instantly recognizable as being related by inversion to bars 1–2; bars 5–8

transpose the melody of bars 1–4 up a third with a modification in bar 8; and in bars 9–10 material derived from bars 6
and 7 is placed at the beginning of a phrase, so that what
were originally the second and third bars in the metrical
structure are transformed into the first and second—this is
variation achieved by metrical means. Those who, in the
heat of musico-aesthetic battle, decried Brahms's "formal"
motivic development as "empty" or "poverty-stricken" in
content were quite wrong, however. It is precisely the consequences, the events to which it leads, that first give color
and character to the modest little motive that opens op. 8
and, far from being overstretched in the process of development, it expands accordingly. The emphasis given by the
transposition in bars 5–8 and the intervention of the metrical variation in bars 9–10 are expressive traits which are the
result of the motivic evolution, that is, of a "formal" procedure. (See example below.)

The spinning of broad melodic paragraphs out of one small motive can become monotonous, however, no matter how variously the material is presented, unless it is alleviated and balanced by constant harmonic variety. The enrichment of the fundamental bass is the correlative, both technically and aesthetically, of developing variation. (In op. 8 Brahms begins with a persistent pedal point and does not begin to enrich the harmony until bars 17–20, when the effect is explosive; this is a special form of differentiation, not simplicity. The pedal point does not represent further simplification of harmonies that are poor in themselves but complication—like a kind of additional dissonance.) However, the enrichment of harmony by increasing the number of degrees in regular use endangers periodic structure as it was understood in about 1800, when its harmonic foundations were simple cadential models such as I–V–V–I or I–(V)II–V–I. (Whether auxiliary degrees and secondary dominants and subdominants are integrated into the model or not, whether they differentiate the pattern or disrupt it and finally destroy it, depends to no small degree on the metrical position of the chord; harmonic analysis is an abstract procedure if no reference is made to the metrical function of the chord.) It is not impossible to encase enriched harmony in a regular periodic structure; as some works by Reger demonstrate, it can be done with violent imperfect and perfect cadences, but the procedure is self-defeating as long as the technical and aesthetic criterion is the rule that development of all the elements of the composition should be analogous.[20] In order to avoid discrepancies between harmony and syntax, Brahms often followed the example of Bach and constructed tripartite groups which owe their form not to the correspondence (motivic analogy and harmonic contrast) of antecedent and consequent clauses but to the evolution of an initial phrase by means of a harmonically enriched developmental passage, not tied down to a quadratic structure, which concludes with a cadential

20. Dahlhaus, *Analyse und Werturteil* (Mainz, 1970), pp. 59ff.

epilogue.[21] (The principal theme of op. 25 is tripartite: the initial phrase comprises bars 1–10, the evolution bars 11–20, and the epilogue, which refers back to the initial phrase without there being any question of ternary form, bars 21–27; but the evolution differs from the typical Bachian procedure of a series of sequences and comes about, as has been shown [p. 49], through the uncommonly differentiated development of a two-note motive, the descending second.) This is not the restoration of something that belongs to the past; it is a derivation or an analogy made under fundamentally different historical conditions.

Different—even contradictory—as the solutions worked out by Brahms on the one hand and by Wagner and Liszt on the other were, it is surely beyond question that their initial problem was the same, arising from the difficulty of reconciling constricted melodic ideas with the desire to work in large forms and from the undermining of classical form by the technical consequences of the brevity of the thematic substance. It is the sameness of the problem which marks the second half of the nineteenth century as an essentially unified epoch in musical history, in spite of the stylistic contrasts it embraced.

4. "Expanded" and "wandering" tonality

The individual elements of musical composition—harmony, counterpoint, motivic technique, and musical syntax —are not mutually independent: each one individually can be described, its functions defined, only with reference to the others and to the effects each has on the others. Any attempt to write a history of harmony which dealt with pitch relationships in isolation would be too abstract to have any useful application: *"schlecht abstrakt"* in Hegel's phrase. Their correlationship makes harmony and syntax inseparable, just as harmony and meter are, or harmony and voice-leading.

21. W. Fischer, "Zur Entwicklungsgeschichte des Wiener klassischen Stils," *Studien zur Musikwissenschaft* 3 (1915): 24–84.

The difference between the Wagnerian (or Lisztian) and the Brahmsian methods of stating and continuing a musical idea caused a divergence in harmonic procedure which has been noted by some commentators, but has never really been studied in the context which gave rise to it. With the Wagnerian procedure of modulatory sequences, chromatic alteration and the undermining of tonality by fragmentation became the principal characteristics of the harmonic writing, while Brahms's use of developing variation, with the enrichment of the fundamental bass, preserved tonal integrity.[22] Later, around 1900, Arnold Schoenberg forced the two trends to come together again, but that does not alter the fact that originally, in the nineteenth century, they represented alternatives: different solutions to the problem of establishing a harmonic technique appropriate to the process of motivic development and the structure of the syntax.

The analyst Schoenberg—whose theoretical conclusions were drawn from the composer Schoenberg's urge to reunite divergent trends—included both Brahms's enrichment of the fundamental bass and Wagner's undermining of tonality in his concept of "expanded .tonality."[23] The weakness of the concept is that it conceals an important difference between the Wagnerian and the Brahmsian techniques, and while the analyses of Brahms on which Schoenberg bases his theses are illuminating, some of his analyses of Wagner are questionable.

If the term "expanded tonality" is given its full value, one of its postulates is that, far from being disrupted or suspended by the Wagnerian procedure of modulation towards some tonally remote region, the listener's awareness of the tonality is actually strengthened by it. For if the formal or syntactical association, the music's inner coherence, is not

22. Schoenberg, *Harmonielehre* (Vienna, 1911), p. 416 [*Theory of Harmony*, trans. R. E. Carter, based on 3rd ed. (1922), London, 1978, p. 370].
23. Schoenberg, *Die formbildenden Tendenzen der Harmonie* (Mainz, 1954), pp. 74 ff. [*Structural Functions of Harmony*, 2d ed., London and New York, 1969, pp. 76ff.].

to become unrecognizable, the listener's tonal awareness is tested and compelled to perceive the tonal relationship of even the remotest excursion. Schoenberg shared with Alfred Lorenz[24] the view that, in Wagner, tonality—the relation, capable of retention by the consciousness, of all harmonic processes to a tonal center—is structural in the wider context. Insofar as this is so, reluctance to hear Wagnerian harmony over long stretches as "centripetal" signifies a rejection of a means of proper formal understanding.

An alternative interpretation of Wagnerian tonality is possible. As they change in quick and often "rhapsodic" succession, the keys, or fragmentary allusions to keys, do not always relate to a constant center, around which they are to be imagined as simultaneously grouped; they should rather be seen as joined together like the links in a chain, without there necessarily being any other connection between the first and third links than the second. In the light of this theory, the characteristic function of Wagner's use of harmony is to establish not hierarchies but an order of succession. This is not to claim that there are no examples in Wagner of tonality which is both "expanded" and yet still clearly related to a tonal center, or even that such examples are rare, but merely that that particular harmonic procedure is not the first that should be cited as representing the principles of Wagnerian form.

If a valid assessment of the merits of these two opposing theories is to be made, it will not be by reference to listeners' reactions (whose validity would have to be measured in turn, thus setting up a vicious circle) but solely by means of formal analysis (though there will still be scope for questioning its intersubjective validity): not, that is, by a psychological process but by a phenomenological one. The question of whether the consciousness needs to retain the sense of a fundamental tonic throughout lon̶g modulatory passages in

24. Lorenz, *Der musikalische Aufbau des Bühnenfestspieles "Der Ring des Nibelungen" (Das Geheimnis der Form bei Richard Wagner,* vol. 1), p. 9.

Wagner will not be decided by reference to statistics about the effects the music has on the listener, but only by an investigation of the formal function of Wagner's use of harmony, and that function will be discovered in the relationship of the harmony and the musical syntax. If the absence of a change of key is irrelevant to the listener's grasp of the form of a particular passage, then the postulate that awareness of the tonic must be retained is shown to be redundant.

Schoenberg[25] interprets an eight-bar passage from Act I of *Tristan*, "War Morold dir so wert", as a tonally integrated period in B minor (with the dominant F♯ minor as an "extension," signifying no change of key):

G♭⁶	C⁶	a♭⁶	e♭⁶	b⁶	C⁶	G⁶		f♯⁴⁶	C♯	f♯
b:V	IIN	VI	III	I	IIN	f♯ : IIN		I⁶₄	V	I
1	2	3	4	5	6			7		8

Schoenberg's analysis is ingenious but not particularly illuminating. Some of his premises are theoretically unsound: it is doubtful whether the listener will hear the reversal of the familiar, well-worn chordal progression IIN–V to V–IIN (bars 1–2) (he will involuntarily hear G♭–C as IIN–V, re-

25. Schoenberg, *Formbildende Tendenzen*, p. 104 [*Structural Functions*, pp. 107f.].

lated to F minor); it is equally doubtful whether he will hear
the chromatic alteration of the roots of the chords VI and III
(bars 3–4). (If the postulate of chromatic alteration of
roots—which rests on a dubious interpretation of the chord
of the Neapolitan sixth and an even more dubious generalization of the outcome of that interpretation—is taken to its
ultimate conclusion, the consequences would be absurd:
every chordal progression could be related to any and every
key.) But above all, Schoenberg's assumption that the passage is harmonically integrated is not born out by formal
analysis. The passage may be eight bars long but its syntactic structure does not rest on a periodic schema representing
a formal correlative to the principle of tonal centrality; it is
created by sequential repetition, a linear and successional
procedure. (Moreover the sequences are real and the inter-
vals equidistant: F–A♭=G♯–B; symmetrical division of the
octave, to which Liszt was particularly prone, is a procedure
alien to tonality and undermines functional tonality:
C–F♯–C; C–E–G♯=A♭–C; C–E♭–F♯–A–C; C–D–E–F♯–
G♯=A♭–B♭–C.) There is admittedly some modification of
the sequences, but there is no difficulty in recognizing the
basic form to which the others must be related if they are to
make sense: the latent original shape I–V is replaced or
"represented" first by IIN–V in F minor, then by I–V^{b3} in
A♭ minor, and finally by I–IIN in B minor. Thus the tonal
fragments are not held together by the persistence of a single
underlying key functioning as a central point of reference
throughout, but by the linear process of sequential repetition, allied to the harmonic reinterpretation of individual
notes, which, being held in common by certain chords, mediate between remote keys or fragmentary tonal allusions.
Thus one expects the A♭ in bar 3 to become the mediant of
F minor (after F minor: IIN–V), and the B in bar 5 to become
the mediant of G♯ minor (A♭ minor); but instead the A♭ acts
as the root of a chord of A♭ minor, and the B as the root of a
chord of B minor.

The tonality characteristic of Wagner, unlike that of
Brahms, is not an "expanded," centripetal one, integrating

remote degrees and regions in one secure tonic to which modulations can always be related, but a "wandering" or "floating" tonality.[26] The fragmentation of classical tonality, with its ability to delineate form across wide spans, into brief tonal particles which follow each other in line, connected like links in a chain rather than assembled round a common center, by no means represents aesthetic weakness, the relinquishment of harmonic function; it is rather the precise correlative of a sense of form which is concerned less with the clearly perceptible grouping of separate parts than with the weaving of an ever denser network of motivic relationships. Wagner envisaged musical form as resembling a woven fabric, as he described it in *Music of the Future,*[27] not an architectural structure. One could refer to it as a dynamic form, which draws the listener into it during its course, whereas one observes an architectural form from the outside. When the listener is sufficiently aware of classical form, all the musical events of a movement can ultimately be perceived in an imaginary simultaneity.

In contrast the tonal centrality created by the enrichment of the fundamental bass and regional connections in the music of Brahms, the complementarity of differentiation and correspondence, express an idea of form that strives for complete and absolute integration—not the integration that comes as a matter of course from following a plan prepared in advance, but integration that must be won, often by force, from recalcitrant material. The structural role of harmony in Brahms is never so much in evidence as where he appears to be adopting Wagnerian and Lisztian expositional procedures but then transmutes them to serve his own idea of form.

The opening of the G minor Rhapsody for piano op. 79, no. 2, appears at first to be a paradigmatic example of the kind of "wandering" or "floating" tonality that is more characteristic of Wagner or Liszt than of Brahms. The first period is tonally unstable, containing fragmentary allusions

26. Schoenberg, *Harmonielehre*, p. 430 [*Theory of Harmony*, p. 383].
27. Wagner, *Gesammelte Schriften*, 7:131f.

to D minor: I–IIN (I merely an upbeat); to F major: V–I; and to G major: IV–VII–I.

It is not imperative but it is possible to relate all these tonal fragments to G minor: for one thing G minor is, so to speak, their common denominator, and for another the chromatic motion through the fourth, D–E♭–E–F–F♯–G, pointing towards G minor, provides the melodic framework (Heinrich Schenker would have called it an *Urlinie*, if he had permitted an ascending *Urlinie*) of the chordal succession. However, the fact that it continues in bars 5–8 as a real sequence transposed a major third upwards disturbs the listener's consciousness of the tonality: centrality has been replaced by linearity. At the end of the principal thematic group (the rhapsody is in sonata form) there is a faint suggestion of G minor (bars 11–12) as a chromatic variant of the G major of bars 9–10; the second subject group is in the key of the dominant, D minor. If the principal key is merely hinted at in the exposition section, it is fully expounded, contrary to convention, in the development section (bars 61–85).

The sequential construction and the tonal instability of the opening spring from the paradoxical formal concept of a sonata-form rhapsody. To begin with, the tonality is allowed to float in a rhapsodic fashion, later it is pinned down by the conventions of sonata form.

Although the principal subject group recalls the expositional procedures of Wagner and Liszt in its syntax and tonality—and in the correlation of sequential structure and "wandering" tonality—it must bear a different interpretation from what would be appropriate in a music drama or a symphonic poem. The fact that G minor can be taken for the common denominator of the tonal fragments in bars 1–4 of the rhapsody is of essential importance for considerations of musical form. (Schoenberg's analogous interpretation of the eight-bar passage from Act I of *Tristan*—the B minor that Schoenberg posited as the underlying tonic is also a common tonal denominator—was wrong, as has been shown, insofar as it mistook the formal nature of the period.) The opening of the rhapsody, at first sight "roving"—to use Schoenberg's alternative to "wandering"—in obedience to no laws, demands to be interpreted tonally because the work is in sonata form (in the nineteenth century sonata form became virtually second nature to listeners with any sense of form). After the advent of the second subject group, which is in the dominant (to be more precise: the key of which is unambiguous and is recognized as the dominant because experience has taught that second subjects are normally in the dominant), it is possible to look back and recognize the opening as the principal subject group, and the scattered suggestions of G minor coalesce, under the influence of formal awareness, to form a tonic. The listener's understanding and recognition of formal conventions intervene in his grasp of the harmony; "rhapsody" is made subject to "sonata form."

5. The "individualization" of harmony

In the sonata, harmony and rhythm are the pre-eminent structural forces, the themes are the material and in the classical sonata they are of less value. There is a real distinction to be made here between an active and a passive role for thematic material, dominant and active in fugue, subservient and suffering—even to the point of suffering deprivation—in the sonata, while harmony and rhythm have priority.[28]

The kind of musical form outlined here by August Halm is the "architectural" variety based on the equilibrium of the parts—which is all that Halm means in this passage by "rhythm"; the equilibrium is observed in all stages of construction, from single bars to the outline of entire movements. (Whether the thesis is valid for the "sonata" in general—for the type, divorced from any particular historical manifestation; whether it applies equally to Beethoven's sonata form, of which Halm was thinking in the passage quoted, and to Mozart's, of which Halm held a low opinion; and whether the release of the themes from structural obligations in Mozartian sonata form did not actually enhance the melodic growth rather than cause it "deprivation"— these are questions that need not be answered here: by his equivocal use of the word "value" Halm equates the function fulfilled by an element of musical form with its aesthetic rank.)

The decline of "quadratic" syntax, the trend towards "musical prose" in the later nineteenth century, was the reverse face, or correlative, of a change in the function of musical thematic writing, which now took the place of "harmony and rhythm" as the primary structural principle (and in the twentieth century, in the music of Schoenberg, became the only structural principle). In order to do justice to the changed musico-historical circumstances, Halm's formula has to be reversed. The loss of structural significance suffered by rhythm (syntax) and harmony did not mean, however, that they became weaker or poorer in themselves but quite the contrary, they became richer. The breakdown or dissolution of quadratic rhythmic (syntactic) structure introduces greater subtlety (not in function but in substance—in respect of the isolated musical event and its

28. A. Halm, *Von zwei Kulturen der Musik,* 3d ed. (Stuttgart, 1947), p. 117.

momentary effect): since the musical structure is no longer determined primarily by the equilibrium of complementary (whether analogous or contrasting) elements, symmetry is no longer obligatory. (It must be admitted that aesthetic quality can suffer if irregular phrases are regarded as self-sufficient, irreducible entities rather than as modifications and transitional forms within a "quadratic" framework: subtlety in one direction is purchased by the loss of refinement in another.) And just as the tendency towards the "direct," prose-like formulation of musical ideas, untrammeled by the need for symmetry, enabled syntax to break free of regular, strophic structures, so harmony, too, was liberated from the traditional formulas and conventions, reused incessantly with occasional minor modifications, which could hardly be avoided so long as harmony had an important structural function to fulfill, as defined by Halm.

At the beginning of the nineteenth century simple patterns of key relationships, constructed on cadential models and with a recurrent generic similarity, provided the basis of all musical forms. But in the second half of the century, in the music of Wagner and Liszt—and in that of Brahms too in some respects—the role of harmony was almost completely reversed. In Wagnerian harmony, with its reliance on chromatic alteration and its consequent tendency towards "wandering" or "floating" tonality (that is, a linear succession of fragmentary allusions to keys), the accent falls on harmonic details—on single chords or unusual progressions—and there is such a degree of differentiation in the compositional technique (the interrelationship of harmony and instrumentation) that it is no exaggeration to speak of an individualization of harmony, which is hardly less important than that of thematic and motivic material. Some harmonic progressions and even some individual chords in Wagner have the same significance as a leitmotiv: the "mystic chord" in *Parsifal*, the expressive and allegorical functions of which were described by Alfred Lorenz,[29] or the

29. Lorenz, *Der musikalische Aufbau von Richard Wagners "Parsifal"* (*Das Geheimnis der Form bei Richard Wagner*, vol. 4), pp. 29ff.

major seventh chord which provides the greater part of the
substance of the Day motive in *Tristan*. Relieved of the
responsibility for the large-scale formal structures, the harmony serves instead to establish the unique identity of one
instant in the music.

The structural function and the individualization of harmony represent alternatives which can, in particular cases,
be reconciled. It is characteristic of Brahms—"the conservative" whom Schoenberg nevertheless hailed as "the progressive"—that on the one hand, as the contemporary of Wagner
and Liszt, he strove to give harmonic details "unique identity," while on the other hand, as a composer who had made
the tradition of Beethoven his own by exploring it from
within, he did not wish to sacrifice the structural function
that tonal harmony could perform over a wide expanse.
There are times when Brahms succeeds not merely in pre-
serving a precarious balance between the two contradictory
tendencies but in actually making one of them the natural
outcome of the other.

The D minor Piano Concerto op. 15 begins with an expansive and harmonically exploratory sequential passage
(bars 1–24), at first sight analogous to the openings of Wagner's *Tristan* prelude and Liszt's *Hamlet*. But the purpose of
sequential writing is different in Brahms from what it is in
Wagner or Liszt. The opening of *Tristan* is harmonically
"centrifugal": it is true that, in spite of the modulation of
the sequences into tonally remote regions, one senses a relation to an A minor which nonetheless remains unheard, but
all the time the movement is away from any center. But although the Brahms op. 15 begins on the tonal periphery the
music's sole ambition is to reach its center (it does so in bar
25, but the tonality is established tentatively rather than
triumphantly): the harmony is "centripetal."

A precedent for this procedure of establishing the tonic by
approaching it from the outside inwards is to be found in the
first subject of Beethoven's Piano Sonata op. 53, the "Wald-
stein." But in Brahms the harmonic details go far beyond the

simple cadential schema followed by Beethoven. The first chord, prolonged over no fewer than ten bars, seems at first to be the inversion of a foreign dominant seventh chord (D–F–Ab–Bb), but the context, its position before the first inversion of the true dominant seventh (C♯–E–G–A), makes it quite clear (even if only retrospectively) that it is the inversion of the augmented sixth chord (i.e. D–F–G♯–Bb): this is a chord which, according to the letter of convention, cannot be inverted, so its inversion signifies an individualization of the harmony. Understood as D–F–G♯–Bb, the first chord acquires a "unique identity," which it owes to its function in the gradual presentation or establishment of the tonic.

The dominance of the idea of originality before all else affected even the use of harmony, which underwent a radical alteration in its formal significance during the later nineteenth century. The emphasis shifted from the general and structural to the particular and instantaneous, from providing a framework, which was its principal function in Mozart and, still, in Beethoven, to the individual characterization of detail, the harmonic "idea." That Brahms nonetheless achieved integration of tonality and syntax—partly, it must be admitted, through the construction of tripartite groups, remotely analogous to Bach's typical continuation procedure, that is, not always derived from the classical model of symmetrical periodic structure—is the outcome of "conservative" resistance to the "tendency of the material," as Adorno would call it. Brahms must surely have felt that tendency and he was sometimes able to do it justice, as at the beginning of his op. 15, where he individualized the harmony by working with (rather than against) formal harmonic functions.

6. Conclusion

So long as one is not afraid of making broad generalizations, fastening on the salient points in tendencies and constructing "ideal types"—and the writing of any kind of history would be severely impeded if methods which have a footing in the empirical but venture beyond its frontiers are to be condemned on principle—it becomes clear that the music of the middle and later nineteenth century is conditioned by the close and intricate relationship between the aesthetic principles and the technical compositional issues that have been examined in the foregoing. These are the pre-eminence of originality, the shrinking of thematic material in inverse proportion to the ambition to create larger forms, the recession of classical periodic structures and of architectural methods of construction based on the principle of equilibrium and exemplified in large-scale metrical patterns, the conversion of developmental techniques like developing variation and real, modulatory sequence to expositional uses, and finally the "individualization" of harmony, which was now liable to produce either superabundant chromaticism resulting in "floating" or "wandering" tonality or else tonal integrity achieved by means of centripetal harmony and enriched fundamental basses. These factors amount to a problem nexus which provides a single, unified background to the music of the whole epoch, far outweighing the significance of stylistic differences and the partisanship of composers and their adherents.

This is not to deny the existence of "external" factors, or to detract from the significance of the effect they had on the development of music. As has already been said, there is no intrinsic technical explanation in the history of composition for the general trend of the music of the second half of the nineteenth century towards ever larger, monumental forms; and there can be no doubt that a sociological study of the audiences which lent their support variously to the musical and musico-political institution established in Bayreuth[30] and to Brahms's chamber music[31] would be not merely per-

---

30. W. Schüler, *Der Bayreuther Kreis* (Münster, 1971).
31. K. Stahmer, *Musikalische Formung in soziologischem Bezug: Dargestellt an der instrumentalen Kammermusik von Johannes Brahms* (diss., Kiel University, 1968).

tinent: it is urgently needed. That there are social implications in the works themselves, in the very conception of the *Ring* and in the idea of absolute music embodied in the string quartet,[32] cannot seriously be denied, although the prospect of deciphering them is one to daunt any scholar whose ambitions go beyond facile categorizations (such as "bourgeois culture") on the one hand and the construction, on the other, of merely verbal analogies, analogies which rest exclusively on the words and not on the matters that they are supposed to represent.

It is accepted that a history of music which examines the subject primarily from the standpoint of compositional issues is one-sided and requires augmentation. The aesthetic and technical terms of reference are inadequate in their exclusiveness but they are equally essential, as a first stage that must on no account be skipped over. However, while it has always been asserted that the fragmentary nature of such description results in an intolerable distortion of the reality it is intended to describe, because one should encompass the whole in order to grasp the individual detail, there has never been any really illuminating substantiation of the claim. (The fundamental rule of hermeneutics, the platitude that the context must always be taken into consideration, remains a shadowy ideal so long as there is a shortage of suitable criteria to help one to decide in any individual case just how large the context is that one needs to consider if one is to come up with a meaningful explanation or interpretation of one particular phenomenon; in any event, the assumption that the context of musical works is always society as a whole is an exaggeration, dogmatic in origin.) The nexus of aesthetic and technical issues that has been outlined here is only part of the history of music in the later nineteenth century, a subject which cannot adequately be reduced to the history of compositional technique in the period. However, the "totality" invoked by methodologists, sitting in judg-

32. Dahlhaus, "Brahms und die Idee der Kammermusik," *Neue Zeitschrift für Musik* 134/9 (1973): 559ff.

ment on studies that are confined to only one, or some, of the aspects of a historical period, is a demand that has not yet been met, and all its attractions do not amount to a guarantee that it ever can be met to a degree consistent with scholarly requirements.

On the other hand the attempt to discover the common ground underlying the contradictions and differences in the music of the later nineteenth century is by no means an endorsement of the dogmatic claim that what unites, what is common to things is *a priori* more important and has a more general significance than what separates and distinguishes them, that foundations amount to more than the building that rises on them. When trying to comprehend a period in the history of ideas, one must resist the temptation to award the homogeneity of the problems posed priority over the multiplicity of the solutions that were explored, if the only reason for doing so is the powerful tradition that encourages historians to reveal the inner coherence behind the contradictions that rend an epoch. Tracing divergent trends back to their common root is not the only way of relating them to each other comprehensibly: like a primary unity, a polarity can also be understood and explained as an ultimate instance, fundamental, irreducible, and meaningful in itself. So far as the history of music in the later nineteenth century is concerned, however, any eventual need to progress beyond the reconstruction of a fundamental unity of compositional issues underlying the stylistic polarities—in the full expectation of discovering new contradictions in a lower stratum—is not yet in sight.

Nationalism and Music

❧

The history of ideas is held in suspicion by materialists, on the grounds that it is liable, either intentionally or innocently, to turn reality upside down. Even the most orthodox of Marxists, however, can hardly deny that there are some ideas which are not exhausted by the function of being a reflection and a vehicle of economic and social structures and processes. While they may be reducible, in the final analysis, to economic and social terms, such ideas are imbued with an independent existence and significance which may be illusory but nevertheless gives them the power to intervene positively in historical developments. Although an outside observer (as opposed to one whose understanding and interpretation have been formed from within) can see the associations between ideas and particular interests, that is, can recognize their "ideological" tendency, that does not justify condemning them as conceptual phantoms which must be expelled from a history based on facts. Ideas are historical facts too. A historian who distrusts "ultimate" causes and single explanations, because they obviously have more to do with the explainer's desire for simplicity than with the true nature of the matter in hand, need not suffer any methodological twinges of conscience if he confines himself to describing nexuses instead of attempting reductions. He can perfectly well expound the relations between economic, social, aesthetic, and technical musical factors and the ideas current at the time, without being obliged in addition to commit himself, as a matter of principle, to adopting any particular hierarchy of points of view—to an affirmation of the invariable primacy of cultural history over sociological interpretations, or vice versa. The notion that he must make a metaphysical confession of some kind—for this is what it amounts to—is an imposition that he has every right to refuse. (If he holds aloof from the battle over "ultimate" principles, it naturally does not mean that he abrogates the right to ascribe greater importance to one factor rather than another, when he has arguments rather than axioms to support his view: eclecticism has always been the philosophy of historical studies and no historian need be ashamed of it.)

1. The *"Volksgeist"* hypothesis

There is hardly a historian left, whether bourgeois or socialist,[1] who still resists the view that the concept of nationality—in music as in other fields—is not an invariable constant but something which alters in response to historical factors. But one of the factors in the nineteenth century which influenced the expression of nationality in music was the idea of nationalism, an idea for which it can be claimed without exaggeration that it not merely created a concept out of existing elements—things that separately could be defined as national—but that it also intervened in the existing situation and changed it (instead of merely interpreting it). Like historicism, a theoretical approach to music which influenced its historical development, nation-

1. Z. Lissa ("Über den nationalen Stil in der Musik," in *Aufsätze zur Musikästhetik*, Berlin, 1969, p. 239) exaggerates when she claims that Marxist historians are the only ones to have placed nationalism in its historical context; some liberal bourgeois historians, such as Hans Kohn, are also in no doubt as to the historical circumstances limiting and affecting the phenomenon.

alism had a retroactive effect on the facts of which it was, or purported to be, the reflection. Adoption of the theory that nationality, the collective spirit of a people, was the most profound motive force in history was partly responsible for creating the phenomenon on which the theory was based—as the example of the "national" interpretation of folk music will show. (There is more to a musical fact than its physical foundations, its acoustic substratum. It has always been formed categorially; and in the nineteenth century the categories that influenced the constitution of the facts of an aesthetic case included the idea of nationalism, which can therefore be said, without turning reality upside down, to have assisted in creating musical facts.)

The word "nationalism" is not being used pejoratively but simply descriptively, as in works of political history. It designates a belief which, in the course of the nineteenth century from the French Revolution to the outbreak of the First World War (or, in the history of music, from the *Eroica* to *Das Lied von der Erde*) became the governing idea without always being held by those in government: the belief that it was to his nation—and not to a creed, a dynasty, or a class—that a citizen owed the first duty in a clash of loyalties.[2] (The socialist nationalism which has gradually displaced bourgeois nationalism since the Mexican revolution of 1910 is an ambiguous phenomenon, if one postulates a clearcut hierarchy of loyalties.)

In the bourgeois nationalism of the nineteenth century, the political element—the claim to the citizen's first loyalty—mingled with the idea, originally formulated by Johann Gottfried Herder, that it was "the spirit of the people" (*der Volksgeist*) which formed the truly fundamental, creative, and stimulating element in art as in other human activities. According to this idea, for instance, it was the spirit of the people of Norway that demanded musical expression in and through Edvard Grieg, and not Grieg (as an

2. H. Kohn, *Die Idee des Nationalismus* (Frankfurt am Main, 1962), pp. 17f.

individual rather than as the representative of his nation)
who first created what is thought to be quintessentially
Norwegian in music.[3] Do individual characteristics proceed
out of the national substance, or is the concept of what is
national formed by generalization on the basis of individual
characteristics? (In the latter case, the concept is necessarily
formed at a secondary stage, but it is no less an "aesthetic
fact" for that.)

It would be a grave distortion of the role that the *"Volksgeist"* hypothesis played in the history of music to allow an
unbalanced emphasis to fall on folk music and the interest
that the folklorists began to show in it. What is far more
characteristic of the nineteenth century is the idea that the
national spirit which manifested itself in folk music at an
elementary level was the same spirit which finally produced
classicism—a national classicism. The musical classicism
of the late eighteenth century was regarded primarily as
German, not as a universal style embracing French and Italian composers as well. The enthusiasm for folk music and
the aspiration to classicism were complementary, not contradictory. Classicism was seen as the final, perfect expression of something which first took shape in folk music; the
noble simplicité of the classical style represented the
simplicity of folk music, renewed and transformed.

Nationalism in fact underwent a profound alteration during the nineteenth century. In the first half of the century
the "nationalist" was also, perhaps paradoxically, a
"cosmopolitan," a "citizen of the world." But after 1849 nationalism adopted a haughtily exclusive or even aggressive
stance, and although it was the oppressors who initiated this
unhappy change and were the primary offenders under it,
the attitude of the oppressed was equally affected by it. So
long as nationalist movements supported the aspirations of

3. A. Einstein (*Die Romantik in der Musik,* Munich, 1950 [*Music in the
Romantic Era,* New York, 1947], p. 349) inclines to the view that a national
style is, to a considerable extent, an individual style appropriated *a pos-
teriori* by national feeling.

every other nation to the freedom from internal and external tyranny that they sought for their own, their horizons were cosmopolitan; Polish nationalism was a "matter of European concern," and Michelet, the "high priest" of liberalism, even spoke in terms of a *"fraternité des patries."*[4] In its later guise, nationalism was introverted and xenophobic, and fostered policies favoring national aggrandizement— policies that were regarded as "realistic" by comparison with the "idealistic" fancies of "cosmopolitanism." In the second half of the nineteenth century nationalism did not draw support and encouragement from the development of other nations, but regarded it as a threat.

In the sphere of music, late Wagner has been accused of aggressive nationalism; although there are some grounds for the charge it is not altogether a just one. (Some particularly sensitive critics have even believed that they could detect in certain passages in his work a musical expression of *Machtpolitik* and an affinity between what is aesthetically overpowering in his music and the use of force in spheres far removed from aesthetics.) But in 1851, in *Opera and Drama*, Wagner was still arguing against the "nationalist trend," which in his view was inimical to "the general human lot" (*das Allgemeinmenschliche*) and served the interests of the old order.[5] In the terminology of Wagner's cultural and philosophical writings, "national," "historical," and "conventional" formed a grouping which he compared unfavorably with "natural" and "original."

Most nineteenth-century composers tried to effect a compromise between cosmopolitan ideas, which had not faded altogether, and their own sense of national identity, which was something that none of them could ignore in the climate of the times. Even after the mid-century, and in spite of the inducements to support the more aggressive form of nationalism, the "national schools" in general pre-

4. H. Kohn, "Begriffswandel des Nationalismus," in *Merkur* 198 (1964):704.

5. Wagner, *Gesammelte Schriften*, 3:259ff.

served a cosmopolitan outlook, insofar as they had no intention that the national music which they created or felt
themselves on the way to creating should be excluded from
universal art (a difficult thing to define); on the contrary, the
national character of their music was what would ensure for
it a place in universal art (rather as Hegel's "spirits of the
peoples" partook of the "world spirit"). The national substance of Russian or Czech music was a condition of its in-
ternational worth, not an invalidation. And it would surely
be inappropriate to say "coloring" instead of "substance"
and "commercial success" instead of "worth"; of course the
charms of the foreign and the picturesque played a part, but
unless there is nothing more to those charms than a passing
novelty—and that is hardly a suitable term to use of
nineteenth-century Slavonic music—they must partake to
some minimal degree in the basic elements of a common
world understanding, that is, they must be "substantial." At
first sight the foreign and the familiar would seem to exert
diametrically opposite attractions, but in fact they con-
tradict and counteract each other far less than they support
and enhance each other: an exotic setting and coloring only
afford clearer definition and vividness to the familiar common elements. The German prehistory which Wagner chose
as the setting for his representation of "the general human
lot" is just such an exotic locale.

It was not the principle of reconciling a national with a
cosmopolitan outlook that caused contention between
nineteenth-century composers (at least, not as long as they
were writing music), but merely the precise relationship between the two. Schumann, for instance, in a review he wrote
in 1836, praised Chopin's "strong and original nationality";
he meant that the national character expressed in Chopin's
music was authentic, because it was the composer's own
("original") nationality, not assumed, as if a non-Pole wrote
"in the Polish manner." But he also said that "the little interest of his native soil has had to be sacrificed to the cosmopolitan interest, and the overly special Sarmatic physiognomy is

already less pronounced in his more recent works."[6] It is not that Schumann would have thought of the universal and the national as mutually exclusive alternatives (and the accuracy or otherwise of the statement as a judgment of Chopin is beside the point). Rather than paraded as a "little interest," as something isolated and insular, national traits should be absorbed into the universal, the cosmopolitan, but they should by no means be extinguished. His national origins ("original nationality") should constitute a source of energy, a substance on which the creative artist can feed, but they should not be his ultimate aesthetic authority. In other words, nationality as such, which is perfectly reconcilable with cosmopolitanism, is not what Schumann would have wanted to see "sacrificed," but the narrow nationalism that through fear or arrogance is incapable of looking further than itself.

Nationalism, the belief in the spirit of a people as an active creative force, is an idea with a character and a function which it is simplistic to identify with the phenomenon of a national style: in other words, they will not be successfully pinned down by the mere act of describing tangible musical characteristics. Distinct national styles can be discerned in polyphonic music from the thirteenth century onwards, although the outlines are dim to begin with and although the concept of nationality has undergone some changes. But it was only during the nineteenth century, only after the French Revolution, that nationalism came to dominate Europe as a mode of thought and a structure of feeling.

If applied rigorously, however, a distinction between national style as a musical fact and nationalism as a creed imposed on music from without is far too crude to be an accurate reflection of the historical and aesthetic reality. For a musical fact is not something pieced together from precise, unambiguous components but the result of the categorial formation of an acoustic substratum, a formation which

6. R. Schumann, *Gesammelte Schriften über Musik und Musiker*, ed. H. Simon (Leipzig, 1888), 1:188.

presupposes or includes aesthetic and ideological elements as well as structural and syntactical factors. Nothing gives a historian who does not subscribe to any particular aesthetic dogma the right to declare an ideological factor, such as nationalism in music, to be *a priori* "non-aesthetic." If a piece of music is felt to be characteristically national, that is an inseparable feature of the work, not something extraneous.

It is no doubt possible to distinguish between central and peripheral elements in the complex which it is convenient to call the "aesthetic features," but nothing would be gained by denying the peripheral elements any part at all in the whole. Moreover the criteria according to which the distinctions are made are not fixed and immutable—the assumption that what is structural is central and what is affective is peripheral is misleading—but are dependent on changing historical, regional, and social circumstances. In a national anthem such motivic work as exists is of slight aesthetic significance and the most important element is the expression of national pride and emotion. But one would be on slippery ground if one described that element as something "extra-musical," because "extra-musical" is not a descriptive term, as it may seem, but a normative one which implies a negative judgment made from the standpoint of a one-sided aesthetic—Hanslick's aesthetic theory of the "purely musical." The concept of what constitutes music is a historically changing category, and it is a principle of historical justice that phenomena should be measured by their own standards, not alien ones. If program music is judged according to the formalistic concept of music, the verdict has been pronounced before the case has even been argued; the implications of the terminology have already condemned it. Much the same applies to the idea of nationalism as an aesthetic factor; if a composer intended a piece of music to be national in character and the hearers believe it to be so, that is something which the historian must accept as an aesthetic fact, even if stylistic analysis—the attempt to "verify" the aesthetic premise by reference to musical features—fails to produce any evidence. There is no line of argument which would make it permissible to leave ideological "appearances" out of account in assessing the aesthetic "reality."

The national significance or coloring of a musical phenomenon is to no small degree a matter of the way it is received by audiences,[7] and that too is a relevant "fact." A piece of folk music, interpolated in a context of polyphonic art music, is by no means essentially "national"; the hearers may well receive it in the light of a primarily social or regional point of view, as a picturesque example of the art of the lower classes or of the population of some faraway place. It was not until the age of nationalism that folk art came to be regarded as a national, rather than a regional or social, phenomenon. But although the interpretation put on the work of art is a secondary consideration it has to be taken into account as one of the aesthetic features: to separate the "facts" of the music, the work "in itself," from the spirit in which it is received under the influence of nationalism would require an act of metaphysical violence.

On the other hand a national style cannot usefully be defined as the sum of the common attributes of all the works written by composers who belong to the same nation—especially in view of the number of composers whose musical nationality is a matter for debate (in cases like Liszt and Handel, it is not necessarily the same as their ethnic nationality).[8] Mechanical inductive processes are already of questionable value in the definition of stylistic epochs (is musical classicism nothing more than a compendium of the common characteristics of the works of Haydn and Pleyel, Mozart and Koželuch?) and they are completely inadequate when it comes to national styles. It seems rather—although there has to be some basis in stylistic fact—that what does

7. Z. Lissa, "Über den nationalen Stil in der Musik," p. 230.

8. A. Einstein, *Nationale und universale Musik* (Zurich, 1958), pp. 236ff.

and does not count as national depends primarily on collective opinion.

In the nineteenth century this opinion was affected by the idea of nationalism insofar as the *"Volksgeist"* hypothesis influenced people, without their being very conscious of it, firstly to inject national sentiments into what were originally neutral stylistic means (e.g. characteristics of musical landscape painting common to all European music), secondly to replace or transform the previously primarily regional or social character of folk music by receiving and interpreting it in a national spirit, and thirdly to single out national traits—which were discernible in music in earlier centuries too, without receiving any special attention—as the essential and fundamental qualities. Taken to its logical conclusion, though in fact no nationalist ever went so far, this process might have led to the self-evidently absurd assertion that the differences between Chopin's ("national") mazurkas and his ("non-national") waltzes are far more important than their similarities.

Thus the phenomenon of national musical style is so closely fused in the nineteenth century with the idea of nationalism—with the hypothesis of the spirit of the people as an active and creative substance and source of energy—that any attempt to enforce a rigid separation of "stylistic" and "ideological" elements would be not only impossible but also inappropriate.

It is customary among students of the period to restrict the concept of musical nationalism to the so-called national schools, which consciously sought to separate themselves from the Italian, French, and German traditions and put themselves on an equal footing.[9] (The strength of the French and Italian influences is generally underestimated in this re-

9. D. J. Grout, *A Short History of Opera*, 2d ed. (New York, 1965), pp. 454ff.; A. Einstein (*Die Romantik in der Musik*) summarizes the development of the German, French, and Italian traditions as "universalism within a national framework" (pp. 234ff.), while he assembles the "national schools" under the umbrella heading of "nationalism" (pp. 343ff.).

spect.) It is a restriction which does not really stand up to scrutiny, for in spite of all the different degrees and variations in its manifestations, the bourgeois nationalism of the nineteenth century was a pan-European phenomenon, and there is as much justification for including *Der Freischütz*, *La muette de Portici*, and *Nabucco* in a list of works whose conception or reception were influenced by nationalism as there is for including *Ivan Susanin*, *Halka*, and *Bánk bán*. And it is precisely Russian, Czech, Hungarian and Norwegian historians of music who should be particularly sensitive about the concept of a "national school," for the very expression implies, tacitly but unmistakably, that "national" is an alternative to "universal" and that "universality" was the prerogative of the "central" musical nations. The term "national school" is a covert admission that the phenomenon it describes is peripheral. (The word "school" is in any case ill-chosen, because the school of the "national" composers was in point of fact not a national one, but the German one, insofar as they did not, like some'of the Russians, do without schooling altogether.)

On the other hand serious consideration should be given to the possibility that the different manifestations of musical nationalism were affected by the types of political nationalism and the different stages in political evolution reached in each country: by the difference between those states where the transition from monarchy to democracy was successful (Great Britain, France) and unsuccessful (Russia), or between states formed by the unification of separate provinces (Germany, Italy) and those formed by the secession of new nation-states from an old empire (Hungary, Czechoslovakia, Poland, Norway, Finland).[10] It is uncertain whether there are any correlations, and, if so, whether they are at all significant; as yet hardly any attention has been paid to the possibility of their existence, since musical

10. T. Schieder, "Europa im Zeitalter der Nationalstaaten," in *Handbuch der europäischen Geschichte*, vol. 6 (Stuttgart, 1968), p. 24.

nationalism has been approached almost exclusively from the point of view of writing national histories of music, which have emphasized what is nationally unique or distinctive rather than what is common to many or all European nations. The fact is, however, that as long as descriptions of the unique, distinctive character of the music of one nation do not include comparisons with other manifestations of musical nationalism, the outlines remain imperfectly drawn. The discovery (or the construction, as the case may be) of a national musical character, which was felt to distinguish a nation from the pan-European tradition, was itself a pan-European phenomenon. And the delineation of a national style should begin not by considering how it stands out against the background of a universal European style (which was to no small degree simply a school style) but by comparing it with other national styles and other concepts of what constitutes a national style. National styles differ not only in their substances but also in the ways in which they are national, as well as in the aesthetic, social, and political functions they fulfill.

2. Nationalism and folk music

The concept of nationality, as one of the aesthetic attributes of music, was affected in two ways by nineteenth-century nationalism and the *"Volksgeist"* hypothesis. In some cases interest and attention were focused upon it but in others nationalism actually created it or at the very least moulded it by reinterpretation of existing traditions. In the eighteenth century—a period in which the merits and failings of French and Italian "taste" were the subject of vehement debate—a national musical style was still not so much the ethnic character which a composer inherited at birth as a convention of writing which he could select and exchange for another at will. (There is no justification for calling Hasse's music in the Italian style "imitative," that is, for judging him according to the principle that musical nationality must not be assumed but "original," as Schumann put it; and even Meyerbeer is best grasped according to eighteenth-century categories.) As a convention, with its own recognized repertory of techniques and traits, a national style in music was something defined and comprehensible.

Things were different in the nineteenth century. As the idea that "original nationality" was something that should work in music "from the inside outwards" gained acceptance, the progress it made was exactly matched by the growth in the aesthetic significance of national characteristics and by a simultaneous loss of definition. Berlioz was felt to be a characteristically French composer; but it proved almost impossible to summarize his national traits in terms of recognizable concepts—at all events it was far more difficult than finding appropriate means to describe the "French manner" of the late seventeenth and the eighteenth centuries (the elements of which had originated with the Italian Lully).

One possible way of escape from the labyrinthine difficulties of finding adequate definitions of what constitutes national "substance" in music is offered by the hypothesis that in the nineteenth century—that is, in the age in which it received more emphasis than ever before—the concept of nationality related not so much to substance as to function (though this is contrary to the nationalist interpretation itself, which regarded nationality as a "substantial" element). The difference can be illustrated by the analogy of Bach's sacred cantatas. There are few features (such as the use of quotations from chorales) to distinguish them from his secular cantatas either stylistically or in melodic substance; this is the condition that makes parody possible. Their liturgical function was almost entirely independent of style, as long as the composer did not actually adopt the idiom of the streets; their "operatic" quality gave rise to some criticism but was not prohibited, and although the tendency to equate the spiritual with archaism exercised some influence it never gained the upper hand.

It is possible to regard nationality in a similar light, as a quality which rests primarily in the meaning invested in a piece of music or a complex of musical characteristics by a sufficient number of the people who make and hear the music, and only secondarily, if at all, in its melodic and rhythmic substance. To express it summarily: so long as gypsy music in Hungary was regarded as authentically Hungarian, it *was* authentically Hungarian; the historical error has to be taken at its face value as an aesthetic truth, for it takes a collective agreement to stamp certain traits as national ones, and in the nineteenth century the agreement was influenced by a collective national consciousness represented by the will to assert a national identity. (Distinguishing between the melodic and rhythmic "substance" and the national "function" of a piece of music does not imply that the national element is something "extra-musical" imposed on the "reality" of the music from without. Function is another aesthetic fact whose narrowly formalistic definition by Hanslick is by no means valid for the age as a whole.)

The hypothesis that the "semantic" interpretation of the national element in nineteenth-century music must be based on a "pragmatic" interpretation (in the terminology of linguistics) is not intended to deny or diminish the importance of folk music, which composers might invoke by allusion or by integration into their own style. The clearest expression of musical nationalism was folklorism. However, it is not clear how far the "ethnic raw material" in which nineteenth-century nationalism purported to discover the roots of national musical styles belongs of its original nature in the category of national at all. The assumption that folk music is always and above all the music of a nation—a view which was taken to be self-evidently true in the nineteenth century—is questionable and ill-founded (which has not prevented it from invading the musical history books).

In the uses to which the expression "the people" is put, referring variously to the lower strata of the population and to the nation as a whole, the concept of the lower classes mingles with the idea of nationality.[11] This is a source of further confusion, insofar as nineteenth-century nationalism was not at all an expression of self-awareness on the part of the lower classes but a bourgeois phenomenon, while for the nobility dynastic loyalties counted more than national ones. The appropriation of folk music by the bourgeoisie, in order to reassure themselves that their national feelings had roots and that their own existence therefore had authentic "originality," was an appeal across the social barriers. The view of the life of the "people" as picturesque, as it was seen in the age of Enlightenment, showed an awareness of the barriers, but they were ignored in the romantic evocation of folk ways and folk art as the expression of a deeper layer of human life and experience which had been overlaid by civilization.

According to Walter Wiora the melodic types of European folk music were transmitted and circulated "not among ethnic groups, for the most part, but among cultural and occupational groups such as shepherds or minstrels."[12] Thus the national element (the equation of which with the popular is a misconception that prevents clear understanding) would be in large measure only secondary in importance. It could, of course, be objected that national musical character is hard to define because it is frequently manifested in traits—such as tone-colors or subtle rhythmic and agogic variations—which are very difficult to describe or notate and therefore in academic studies often fail to receive their due weight. (If this were correct, then the impression that nationality has only a small part to play in older folk music might owe less to the true nature of things than to the man-

11. The same applies to the German *das Volk*, which cannot even allow the distinction English makes between "people" in this double sense and the now primarily technical, adjectival "folk," so that the association between terms like *Volksgeist* and *Volksmusik* is even more compelling than that between "the spirit of the people" and "folk music" [*Translator*].

12. W. Wiora, "Über die sogenannten nationalen Schulen der osteuropäischen Musik," in *Historische und systematische Musikwissenschaft* (Tutzing, 1972), p. 340.

ner in which it has been researched.) On the other hand, there is little doubt that until the late eighteenth century, as has been said, it was not national differences but regional and social differences that mattered in folk music, and this is how it would have seemed to the people who made the music as much as to external observers. National consciousness was an exception, even in politics; particular circumstances, such as the Hussite wars of the fifteenth century, might engender it, but otherwise it was a prerogative of the educated and was not found, in particular, among the classes where folk music had its roots. It never entered anyone's head to look upon national characteristics, in the idealized form of "the spirit of the people," as the source and substance of every "authentic" intellectual and artistic activity.

It was the nineteenth century which chose to believe—on very shaky grounds—that national character was the primary and essential quality of folk music (the equation of "primary" with "essential" was a notion of the romantics) and that folk music expresses the spirit of a people (understood as the spirit of a nation, first and most clearly manifested in the culture of the lower classes). At all events these beliefs were not established facts supporting nationalism but pious hopes created by nationalism itself. What is taken to be the premise and substance of nationalism is in fact its consequence and corollary.

Although the national character of folk music is—at least partly—the result of a latter-day, "sentimental" reinterpretation, that does not mean that the feelings and associations linked with it are in any way invalid or unfounded. To treat a feature that emerges at a secondary stage as immaterial is to fall into the trap of assuming that the essence of a thing derives exclusively from its original state. But there is no reason to regard the exterior appearance of a thing as disposable simply because it formed later.

If on the one hand, as it appears (the problems have by no means yet been solved but at least they have been posed, after certain false assumptions have been cleared away), folk music is to no small degree regional or even local in its character and coloring, on the other hand some of the traits which were felt to be specifically national in the nineteenth century actually stretch far across national boundaries. This is a fact which remained concealed because the study of folk music was carried out only on a national level. But to write off the nationalist interpretation of folk music as an aesthetic error which is now being set right by empirical research would also be a mistake: a misuse of the categories. Aesthetically it is perfectly legitimate to call bagpipe drones and sharpened fourths typically Polish when they occur in Chopin and typically Norwegian when they occur in Grieg, even if some historians are irritated by the paradox of something which is common to national music generally and yet is felt to be specifically national in the consciousness of the individual nations. Firstly the national coloring does not reside in separate, isolated traits, but in the context in which they are found. Secondly the aesthetic element, the validity, has to be distinguished from the history of the origin and growth, the genesis: if there is a class of people among whom the music is transmitted and who recognize a body of characteristics as specifically national, regardless of the provenance of the separate parts, then those people constitute an aesthetic authority. Archaisms which diverge from the norms of the universal classical style—like the bagpipe drone and the sharpened fourth—are accepted as national features; the archaic and the national are linked by two things, the *"Volksgeist"* hypothesis and a denial of the universal. Local reinterpretation in this fashion is a historical process and creates its own aesthetic legitimacy.

3. On the aesthetics of national expression in music

It is by no means so self-evident or inevitable that the course of developments in music should be affected by the predominant ideas of the age as has been supposed by historians of ideas (and by some Marxists, who may have "turned the history of ideas the right way up" but nevertheless remain substantially dependent on it). Neither the spirit of the period of political ferment preceding the outbreak of revolution in 1848 nor the naturalism of late nineteenth-century literature left any perceptible traces behind in German music, other than a few quotations of the *Marseillaise*. Besides, the idea that all areas of life are permeated to an exactly equal degree by the spirit of an age comes to grief on the erroneous implication that wherever common or analogous traits recur they are, as a matter of principle, more significant than distinguishing or divergent features. It is easy enough to discover features of Jugendstil or art nouveau in music written around 1900, but they are peripheral not central elements. Contrary to the assumptions of the historians of ideas, the linking, associative elements may be merely epiphenomena.

"External" and "internal" circumstances, general and specifically musical conditions had to coincide in the nineteenth century in order to make it possible for the idea of nationalism to have musical consequences which belong to history, rather than merely to the spoil-heaps of the past. If the technical and aesthetic conditions had not been ripe for it, nationalism would have played no part in the history of music, however great its influence in politics and society. The style of music can be dictated but not its quality.

It is true that at first glance the stage reached in the evolution of compositional technique seems to have been extremely unfavorable. Nationalism took its stand on folk music—and in the nineteenth century, except in Norway, that meant a monodic tradition.[13] How then could it have any significant effect on compositional development in an age when musical progress was regarded as a condition of

13. I. Bengtsson ("Romantisch-nationale Strömungen in deutscher und skandinavischer Musik," in *Norddeutsche und nordeuropäische Musik*, ed. C. Dahlhaus and W. Wiora, Kassel, 1965) rightly stresses that the study of musical nationalism would have to take as its starting point the conception of folk music that was entertained in the nineteenth century, and not the insights gained from modern ethnological studies.

artistic authenticity and was understood before all else as ever greater subtlety of harmonic elaboration? It was only in the twentieth century, with Bartók and Stravinsky, that rhythm and melody were taken as the starting points in mediating between folk music on the one hand and art music's search for novelty on the other. This apparent drawback was in fact an advantage. Folk music was integrated into the context of nineteenth-century harmonic writing, but because it was originally monodic (or performed in heterophonic variants) it resisted assimilation into the well-worn formulas of major-minor tonality; for that very reason it challenged composers to invent unusual harmonies, to make experiments which in turn affected harmony in music unconnected with folk music, and so influenced the mainstream of developments. The experimentation had the advantage, moreover, of having a goal, of being undertaken in response to a specific, well-defined problem.

If harmony which purported to be in the spirit of folk music stimulated musical "progress," it was precisely because it was at odds with the predominant musical tendency, as represented by Wagner. (The same is true to a lesser degree of the "historicist" style of harmony which grew out of the fashion for harmonizing plainsong, a process which left its mark on some of the works of Saint-Saëns.) It provided an alternative, which also had in it the seeds of future development rather than leading up a historical blind alley. The harmonic style of *Tristan*, governed by the dominant and colored by a chromaticism which derives from harmonic ambiguity, is confronted, in works like Grieg's *Slåtter*, with a modally based harmonic style and with a chromaticism determined primarily by melodic, contrapuntal features.

The second precondition which enabled nationalism to intervene in the development of music was aesthetic. The pre-eminent aesthetic principle of the nineteenth century was the dogma of originality, an ideal which gave rise to a constant search for novelty.[14] The seal of aesthetic authenticity was placed only on what was unfamiliar; imitation was no longer, as in the past, applauded as a pious honoring of tradition, of what was "old and true," but condemned as epigonism, the products of which were intellectually disreputable, however faultless they might be technically. (Social historians explain the search for originality in terms of the artists' need to attract attention in the market-place. This has a tempting simplicity but it is hardly the whole truth. When the market-place is catering for mass consumption it requires not only eye-catching originality but also the ceaseless repetition and quarrying of ideas which have already proved successful, whereas the art music of the nineteenth century universally acknowledged the aesthetic principle that a composer must not become his own epigone, something for which social history has not yet provided an explanation.)

But the French Revolution cast a long shadow over the nineteenth century, and art music was also confronted with the obligation to abandon aristocratic and esoteric goals and become democratic and popular. At least in principle—even though it failed to take effect in reality—opera, from Méhul and Cherubini onwards, and the symphony, in Haydn's last works and in Beethoven, addressed themselves to "the people" or "human kind." This lofty and humane principle, enjoining the blending of the significant with the popular, was of course utopian, but that does not alter the fact that it reflected the aesthetic, social, and moral intention which informed both the symphony and revolutionary and romantic opera—genres of musical mass appeal. (There is no reason why Germany should have a monopoly of operatic composers to whom the term "romantic" in the wider sense may properly be applied: as well as Weber, Marschner, and Wagner, their number includes Bellini, Donizetti, and Meyerbeer.)

14. K. von Fischer, "Versuch über das Neue bei Beethoven," in *Kongressbericht Bonn 1970*, pp. 3ff.

This ideal of popularity was obviously in direct opposition to the search for constant novelty enforced by the doctrine of originality; something for which the listener is unprepared, and which requires a certain amount of application to understand, is not simultaneously capable of being appreciated and welcomed by a wider public—or so it would seem. But musical nationalism offered a way of escape from the dilemma, and this is what gave it the power to intervene in the aesthetic situation. Music which was prompted to harmonic experiment by procedures or material originating in folk music was on the one hand technically progressive, thus meeting the requirement of novelty; on the other hand its appeal to national sentiment—or, for foreigners, its picturesque charm—could make it immediately popular. Tinged with folk hues and yet uncompromised in its artistic pretensions, this kind of music seemed to suspend or resolve the conflict between the avant-garde and popular taste. (An idea which was closely associated with the expression of nationality in music and at the same time tried to reconcile artistic integrity with popularity was that of the "appearance of familiarity.")

Nevertheless, the popularity so achieved remained confined to the bourgeoisie: the "spirit of the people" that was thought to speak in the music of the "national schools" was heard only by the educated, not by the "people" themselves. The artistic character of this music was separated from the folk music it invoked by a social gulf which amounted sometimes to a ravine. If Smetana had the tact and sensitivity to refuse to plunder the arsenal of folk music in his search for a "national" style of musical expression, this was probably in part because he was conscious that the "native" folk music of his own country was "alien" to the bourgeoisie and could be invoked only across the social barriers. But when it comes to invoking or imitating a model, folklorism—though nationalist in inspiration—is no different in principle from the exoticism or historicism of the nineteenth century. The process of gathering heterogeneous material from exotic sources and incorporating it into the here and now in art is aesthetically and technically exactly the same whether the remoteness of the sources is regional, social, or historical in kind. (Chauvinist criticism did not prevail upon Bartók to reduce the scope of his exploration of folk music, which went beyond the frontiers of Hungary.) Admittedly it was generally held that the emotions and association generated by one's "own" folk music went "deeper" than those aroused by the exotic and alien; yet there is reason to doubt whether patriotism was a more powerful emotional force in the nineteenth century than the craving for the exotic.

The only logical conclusion to be drawn from the Herderian thesis of the creativity and active historical influence of the *"Volksgeist"* is that the seal of aesthetic legitimacy and authenticity can be conferred solely when the composer uses the folk music of his own nation. To assert, however, that Glinka is "authentic" when he writes pieces of a Russian character, but "inauthentic" when the stimulus is Spanish, would be absurd (and the musical nationalists always avoided making any such claim). In spite of Nietzsche's eloquent argument in its favor, the concept of "authenticity" is a questionable aesthetic category[15] (though admittedly this was not realized until the concept began to lose ground in moral philosophy too). It is no bar to aesthetic success if a composer invokes the musical idiom of a nation other than his own—"from without," so to speak—just as in the eighteenth century, when pieces "in the French style" or "in the Italian manner" were popular. In music, unlike language, work of significance can be created in "broken" Spanish or Hungarian. Aesthetic "rightness" is almost completely independent of folkloristic purism.

Despite this it cannot be denied that the practice of invoking folk music and the routine use of national musical idioms merely to provide coloring were gradually discon-

---

15. T. W. Adorno, "Goldprobe," in *Minima moralia* (Berlin and Frankfurt am Main, 1951), pp. 287ff.

tinued or sank to the level of entertainment music, and this obviously happened under the influence of the principle of originality, which embraced not only the requirement of novelty but also the idea of spontaneity, of "authenticity" (as opposed to the exploitation of ideas, or idioms, originating elsewhere). National character was something to be produced "from within" and not introduced "from without."[16] A national style, embodying the spirit of a people in musical sound, was conceived of as the expression of a form of existence, not merely as something which a composer could arbitrarily adopt and exchange, like a "popular manner," a "conversational manner," or a "salon manner." (The "popular manner," as it was understood in the late eighteenth and early nineteenth centuries, reflected detachment, not identification—by contrast with national style in the positive sense.) One of the differences between the nineteenth century and the age of Enlightenment was that the category of "style" took on "existential" significance. A composer did not choose a style—a convention of writing—but expressed himself in it. Thus the concept of "authenticity," questionable though it may be, changed music history.

16. B. Bartók, "Vom Einfluss der Bauernmusik auf die heutige Kunstmusik" (1920), in *Musiksprachen* (Leipzig, 1972), pp. 155ff.

APPENDIX

Friedrich Nietzsche
ON MUSIC AND WORDS
Translated by Walter Kaufmann

Translator's Note

Since Professor Dahlhaus first published his essay, all of Nietzsche's own musical compositions have finally been published[1]— many of them composed for poems written by others—and at a Nietzsche conference in West Berlin early in 1977 several papers dealt with Nietzsche's relation to music.[2]

It is interesting to relate "On Music and Words" to Nietzsche's own compositions. He himself was one of those "composers who write music for extant lyrical poems" (see the sixth paragraph of Nietzsche's essay). When he rejects the proposition that "the *feeling* generated by the poem . . . gives birth to the composition" and insists instead that "a musical excitement that comes from altogether different regions *chooses* the text of this song as a metaphorical expression for itself," he bases his view on his own experience. Janz says in his notes at the end of his edition of Nietzsche's music, without ever referring to the essay "On Music and Words": "Almost always the musical idea can be shown to have been primary. To fit the text to it, Nietzsche changes it in the case of translations; original German poems he takes over pretty faithfully but presses them uncomfortably under the musical line. It remains striking that he set to music for the most part texts by others, although he had a large number of his own poems at his disposal" (p. 327).

1. Friedrich Nietzsche, *Der musikalische Nachlass*, ed. Curt Paul Janz (Basel, 1976).
2. All of the papers as well as the discussion were published in 1978 as volume 7 of the annual *Nietzsche Studien*.

"Hymn to Friendship" represents the most interesting case. Almost all of Nietzsche's compositions antedate his first book. One can almost say that when he became a writer he gave up composing. But this hymn kept haunting Nietzsche. On May 5, 1873, he wrote his friend Rohde that the hymn "begins *'Freunde, Freunde! haltet fest zusammen!* [Friends! Friends! Stick together firmly!]' I have not got any further than this with the poem, but the hymn is finished—and here is the metrical scheme: ..." And: "Prize contest for all of my friends: to write one or two stanzas like that!" As Janz comments, "Here, too, the music is there before the text!" (p. 339).

Here was perhaps the greatest and—in the long run—the most influential German poet of the second half of the nineteenth century asking his friends, who were not poets, to write a text for his hymn! He could not write an adequate text for his music any more than he could write music for his best poems.

In the summer of 1882 Nietzsche became enormously enthusiastic about Lou Salomé's poem "Prayer to Life" and decided to set it to music—making use of the music he had written for "Hymn to Friendship." "He forces the poem under the pre-existing melody which he adapts only a little. . . . This state of affairs—the composition comes *first,* the adaptation to the text only *later*—is crucial," says Janz (p. 340). Eventually, Heinrich Köselitz, the younger friend whom Nietzsche called Peter Gast, helped to set the poem for chorus and orchestra, and this was the one composition that Nietzsche published: *Hymnus an das Leben* (Hymn to Life, 1887).

The criticism written by poets usually has some reference to their own work. T. S. Eliot is a case in point. The same is true of the criticism written by composers. Both Wagner and Nietzsche show this. It would be rash to jump to the conclusion that this automatically invalidates criticism that is rooted in practice.

The German text of this essay is included in volume III of the *Musarionausgabe* of Nietzsche's *Gesammelte Werke.* It is not to be found in Schlechta's popular edition of *Werke in drei Bänden,* which is in any case inadequate for scholarly work, but in the *Kritische Gesamtausgabe* now in process of publication it appears in volume III.3 (1978).

As in my translations of ten of Nietzsche's books and of some of his other *Nachlass* material, I have tried to recapture his style. I have resisted the strong temptation to bring it closer either to the style of his later works, which I prefer, or to my own way of writing. After all, it is interesting to see how far Nietzsche had to go before he achieved the electric brilliancy of his later style. Nevertheless, some very long sentences have been broken up, and the English version is easier reading than the original German. The beginning of the essay still makes hard reading, at least down to the paragraph that begins: "Anyone who has followed these difficult considerations with some good will, close attention, and imagination, making amends where our expressions are too terse or unconditional. . . ." There are many passages in the original that one has to read several times before one can be at all sure what is meant; but that, of course, is not unusual in German philosophy. What is singular is the clarity Nietzsche achieved in his later works. And even this essay is less difficult and more rewarding than much of the recent literature on the subject. Readers who have tried to fathom Heidegger, Adorno, and Benjamin, should find this essay delightful as well as profound.

The four lines of verse in the penultimate paragraph come from the Prelude to Goethe's *Faust*. The Latin words that conclude the essay come from Horace and mean "this noble pair of brothers."

On Music and Words

What has been said here concerning the relation of language to music must also be true of the relation of the *mime* to *music*, for the same reasons. Compared with the eternal significance of music, even the mime, as the intensified symbolism of human gestures, is merely an allegory that expresses the innermost secret of the music only very externally, by means of the passionate motions of the human body. But let us include language, too, in the category of body symbolism and juxtapose *drama* and music, in accordance with the canon proposed above; then a sentence in Schopenhauer that needs to be taken up again later on, should become perfectly clear: "Although a purely musical person would not make any such demand, and the pure tonal language is self-sufficient and requires no help, it might be all right to add words or even the visual performance of an action to it to ensure that our visual and reflecting intellect, which does not like to be totally idle, should also have a light and analogous occupation. Thus our attention actually sticks to and follows the music more closely, and at the same time what the music is saying in its general and imageless language of the heart is based on a visual image, a schema, as it were, something comparable to an

106

example that supports a general concept. Indeed, this sort of thing will intensify the impression made by the music." (Schopenhauer, *Parerga*, vol. II, "On the Metaphysics of the Beautiful and Aesthetics," section 224). If we ignore the naturalistic, external motivation—that our visual and reflecting intellect does not like to be totally idle while listening to music and our attention is aided by a visual action—then Schopenhauer was absolutely right when he characterized the drama and its relation to music as a schema, as an example versus a general concept. And when he adds, "Indeed, this sort of thing will heighten the impression made by the music," the startling ubiquity and early occurrence of vocal music and of the association of music with images and concepts prove the truth of his insight. The music of every people certainly begins in association with lyrical poetry, and it passes through the most important stages of its development in this company, long before there can be any thought of absolute music. If we understand this primeval lyrical poetry of a people as an imitation of the artistry of nature—and we have no other choice—then we must find the original model of this association of music and lyrical poetry in the *duality* that nature has built into *the essence of language*, which we must now penetrate more deeply, after our discussion of the relation of music and image.

The multiplicity of languages immediately reveals the fact that word and thing do not completely and necessarily coincide and that words are symbols. But what do words symbolize? Surely, only representations, whether these should be conscious or for the most part unconscious. For how could a word-symbol correspond to that inmost essence whose images we ourselves are along with the world? It is only through representations that we know this kernel; we are familiar only with its expression in images; otherwise there is no bridge anywhere that might lead us to the kernel itself. Even the whole realm of drives, the interplay of feelings, sensations, emotions, and acts of will, is known to us

when we examine ourselves most closely—as I must inter-
pose against Schopenhauer—only as representation and not
according to its essence. We may add that even Schopenhauer's "will" is nothing but the most general manifestation of something that is otherwise totally indecipherable
for us.

Although we must bow to rigid necessity and can never
get beyond representations, we can nevertheless distinguish
two major species in the realm of representations. One kind
reveals itself as sensations of pleasure and displeasure that
accompany all other representations as a never-failing
figured bass. This most general manifestation which is our
only clue to all becoming and willing and which we will
continue to call "will" has its own symbolic sphere in language, too. It is as fundamental for language as this manifestation is for all other representations. All degrees of pleasure
and displeasure—expressions of *one* primeval ground that
we cannot see through—find symbolic expression in the
tone of the speaker, while all other representations are designated by the *gesture symbolism* of the speaker. Insofar as
this primeval ground is the same in all human beings, the
tonal background is also universal and intelligible despite
the differences between languages. Out of this develops the
more arbitrary gesture symbolism that is not wholly
adequate to its foundation, and with this begins the multiplicity of languages whose variety we may consider meta-
phorically as a strophic text for this primeval melody of the
language of pleasure and displeasure. We believe that the
whole realm of consonants and vowels may be included in
the symbolism of gestures—consonants and vowels are,
without the crucial fundamental tone, nothing but *positions*
of the language organs or, in brief, gestures. As soon as we
think of *words* as welling up from the mouth of man, the
root of the word is produced first of all along with the foundations of this gesture symbolism, the *tone background*,
which is the echo of the sensations of pleasure and displeasure. As our whole corporeality is related to that primordial

manifestation, the "will," the word that consists of consonants and vowels is related to its tone foundation.

This primordial manifestation, the "will" with its scale of
sensations of pleasure and displeasure, gains an ever more
adequate symbolical expression in the development of
music, and this historical process is accompanied by the
perpetual striving of lyrical poetry to circumscribe music in
images. This dual phenomenon can be found performed in
language from its first beginnings, as has just been shown.

Anyone who has followed these difficult considerations
with some good will, close attention, and imagination, making amends where our expressions are too terse or unconditional, will share certain advantages with us. He will be able
to consider some exciting issucs that are much debated in
contemporary aesthetics and above all by contemporary artists more seriously and to give more profound answers than
is the rule now. Imagine, after all preconditions, what an
undertaking it must be to write music for a poem, that is, to
wish to illustrate a poem by means of music, in order to
secure a conceptual language for music in this way. What an
inverted world! An undertaking that strikes one as if a son
desired to beget his father! Music can generate images that
will always be mere schemata, as it were examples of its real
universal content. But how should the image, the representation, be capable of generating music? Not to speak of the
notion that the concept or, as has been said, the "poetical
idea" should be capable of doing this! While it is certain that
a bridge leads from the mysterious castle of the musician
into the free country of images—and the lyric poet walks
across it—it is impossible to proceed in the opposite direction, although there are said to be some people who have the
delusion that they have done this. Populate the air with the
imagination of a Raphael and contemplate, as he did, how
St. Cecilia is listening, enraptured, to the harmonies of
angelic choirs: no sound issues from this world though it
seems to be lost in music. But if we imagined that this harmony did actually acquire sound by virtue of a miracle,

where would St. Cecilia, Paul, and Magdalen and the singing angels suddenly disappear? We would immediately cease to be Raphael, and even as the instruments of this world lie broken on the ground in this painting, our painter's vision, conquered by something higher, would pale and vanish like shadows.

But how could such a miracle occur? How could the Apollinian world of the eye, wholly absorbed in visual contemplation, be able to generate a tone which after all symbolizes a sphere that is excluded and overcome by the Apollinian abandonment to mere appearance? The delight in mere appearance cannot generate out of itself the delight in nonappearance. The delight of seeing is a delight only because nothing reminds us of a sphere in which individuation is broken and annulled. If our characterization of the Apollinian as opposed to the Dionysian was approximately right, then the notion that the image, the concept, a mere appearance should somehow have the power to generate a tone must strike us as wildly wrong. One should not try to refute us by pointing to composers who write music for extant lyrical poems, for we shall have to insist after all we have said that the relation of lyrical poems to such compositions must at any rate be very different from that of a father to his child. And what sort of relation might it be?

On the basis of a popular aesthetic view some people will try to meet us halfway with the proposition: "It is not the poem but the *feeling* generated by the poem that gives birth to the composition." I cannot agree. Feeling, the faint or strong excitation of the basic ground of pleasure and displeasure, is altogether the inartistic *par excellence* in the realm of creative art, and only its total exclusion makes possible the full self-absorption of the artist and his disinterested contemplation. Here one might object that I myself have only just said of the "will" that in music it attains an increasingly adequate expression. My answer to that is, condensed into an aesthetic principle: *the will is the subject of music but not its origin*, meaning the will in its utmost generality, as the primordial manifestation which includes all becoming. What we call *feeling* is, in relation to this will, already permeated and saturated by conscious and unconscious representations and hence no longer directly the subject of music, much less its generator. Take, for example, the feelings of love, fear, and hope: directly, music cannot do a thing with them because each of these feelings is permeated by and saturated with representations. Yet these feelings can serve to symbolize the music, which is what the lyric poet does when he translates this realm of the "will," which cannot be approached by means of concepts and images and yet is the real content and subject of music, into the metaphorical world of feelings. All who feel, when listening to music, *that the music has an effect on their emotions,* resemble the lyric poet; the distant and remote power of music appeals to an *intermediate realm* in them that gives them, so to say, a foretaste, a symbolical preconcept of the real music, the intermediate realm of the emotions. Of such listeners one might say, regarding the "will" which is the only subject of music, that their relation to this will is like that of the analogical morning dream to the real dream according to Schopenhauer's theory. But to all those who can approach music only by way of their emotions one must say that they always remain in the antechambers and will never gain access to the sanctuary of music which the emotions, as I have said, cannot show but only symbolize.

Regarding the origin of music, I have already explained that this cannot by any means be the "will" but must lie in the lap of the power that in the form of the "will" generates a visionary world: *the origin of music lies beyond all individuation,* and after our discussion of the Dionysian this principle is self-evident. At this point I should like to juxtapose once more very clearly the crucial claims entailed by our treatment of the Dionysian and the Apollinian.

The "will" as the most original manifestation is the subject of music, and in this sense music can be called an imitation of nature, but of the most general form of nature.

The "will" itself and feelings—being manifestations of the will that are already permeated by representations—are totally incapable of generating music, even as music is totally incapable of representing feelings or having feelings for its subject, the will being its only subject.

Those who carry away feelings as the effects of music possess in them, as it were, a symbolic intermediate realm that can give them a foretaste of music while at the same time it excludes them from its inmost sanctuaries.

The lyric poet interprets music for himself by means of the symbolic world of the emotions while he himself is at rest in Apollinian contemplation and above these emotions.

When the composer writes music for a lyrical poem, therefore, he, as a musician, is not excited either by the images or by the feelings speaking through this text. A musical excitement that comes from altogether different regions *chooses* the text of this song as a metaphorical expression for itself. A necessary relation between poem and music thus makes no sense, for the two worlds of tone and image are too remote from each other to enter more than an external relationship. The poem is only a symbol and related to the music like the Egyptian hieroglyph of courage to a courageous soldier. Confronted with the supreme revelations of music, we even feel, willy-nilly, the *crudeness* of all imagery and of every emotion that might be adduced by way of an analogy. Thus Beethoven's last quartets put to shame everything visual and the whole realm of empirical reality. In the face of the supreme deity revealing himself, the symbol no longer has any significance; indeed, it comes to be seen as an insulting externality.

Do not take offense when we include the last movement of Beethoven's Ninth Symphony in our discussion, also from this point of view, and speak very candidly about it, although it is without equal and its magic defies analysis. That Schiller's poem "To Joy" is totally incongruous with this dithyrambic world redemption jubilation and that it is inundated by this sea of flames as if it were pale

moonlight—who would take away from me this most certain feeling? Indeed, who would be able to dispute my claim
that the only reason why this feeling does not find over-
whelming expression when we listen to this music is because the music blinds us totally to images and words and
we *simply do not hear anything of Schiller's poem.* All of
the noble verve, even the sublimity of Schiller's verses,
seems disturbing, distressing, and even crude and insulting
beside the truly naive and innocent folk melody of joy. Only
the fact that one does not hear it as the choir and the masses
of the orchestra unfold ever more fully, keeps us from ex-
periencing this incongruity. What, then, are we to say of the
incredible aesthetic superstition that Beethoven in the
fourth movement of the "Ninth" gave a solemn testimony
concerning the limits of absolute music and thus unlocked
the portals to a new art in which music is said to be able to
represent even images and concepts and has thus supposedly
been made accessible for "conscious spirit"? What does Beethoven say himself when he introduces this choral ode with
a *recitativo*? "O friends, not these sounds, but let us strike
more agreeable and joyous ones!" More agreeable and joyous
ones! For that he needed the persuasive tone of the human
voice; for that he needed the innocent air of the popular
song. Longing for the most soulful total sound of his orchestra, the sublime master reached not for words but for a
"more agreeable" sound, not for concepts but for the sound
that was most sincerely joyous. And how could he be misun-
derstood? Precisely the same characterization that Richard
Wagner gave of the great *Missa Solemnis* applies to this
movement: "a purely symphonic work of the most authentic spirit of Beethoven. . . . The singing voices are treated
here as human instruments, and that is, as Schopenhauer
insisted quite rightly, all they are. Precisely in these great
ecclesiastical compositions, the text that is used is not understood by us in accordance with its conceptual meaning,
but serves in the context of a musical work of art solely as
material for vocal song and does not disturb our musically

oriented feeling, only because it does not prompt any rational representations in us but—quite in keeping with its ecclesiastical character—touches us only with the impression of familiar symbolical formulas of faith." Incidentally, I do not doubt that Beethoven, if he had written his projected Tenth Symphony, for which we have his sketches, would have written the *tenth* symphony.

After these preparations, let us now approach the discussion of *opera* and then proceed afterwards to its counter image in Greek tragedy. What we found in the last movement of the "Ninth," on the highest peaks of the development of modern music—that the content of the words drowns unheard in the general sea of sound—is nothing unique and unusual but the general and eternally valid norm in the vocal music of all ages, and nothing else would accord with the origin of the lyrical song. The individual who is in a state of Dionysian excitement has no *listeners* to whom he has anything to communicate any more than does an orgiastic crowd, while the epic narrator and, more generally, the Apollinian artist does presuppose such a listener. It is of the essence of Dionysian art that it does not know any consideration for a listener; the enthusiastic servant of Dionysus is understood only by his peers, as I have put it earlier. But if we imagined a listener at these endemic outbursts of Dionysian excitement, we should have to predict that he would suffer the fate of Pentheus, the eavesdropper who was discovered and torn to pieces by the maenads. The lyrical poet sings "as the bird sings," alone, prompted by his inmost necessity, and has to fall silent when a listener confronts him with his demands. It would therefore be altogether unnatural to demand of the lyrical poet that one should also understand the words of the text of his song—unnatural because the listener would make demands although he has no rights whatsoever in the face of a lyrical outpouring.

Let us ask in all honesty, with the poems of the great ancient lyricists in our hands, whether they could even have thought that their world of images and thoughts might become clear to the crowd of people standing around them.

Try to answer this serious question with an eye to Pindar
and the choral songs in Aeschylus. These immensely bold
and dark intricacies of thought, this whirlpool of images
that impetuously keeps giving birth to itself, this oracular
tone of the whole that we, *without* the diversion of music
and orchestration, often cannot penetrate even with the utmost attention—this whole world of miracles should have
been transparent as glass for the Greek masses and should
have served as a visual-conceptual interpretation of the music? And Pindar's thought-mysteries should have been intended by the wonderful poet to make clearer the music that
was, taken by itself, compellingly clear?

Surely, this consideration forces us to understand what
the lyrical poet really is, namely, the artistic human being
who must interpret the music *for himself* by means of the
symbolism of images and emotions but who has nothing to
communicate to the listener. Indeed, in his transport he
simply forgets who is standing close to him, listening greed-
ily. And as the lyric poet sings his hymn, the people sing
their folksongs for themselves, prompted by an inner need,
not caring whether the words are understood by those who
do not sing.

Let us think of our own experiences in the elevated fields
of music as a fine art: what did we understand of the text of a
Palestrina mass, a Bach cantata, a Handel oratorio, as long as
we did not join in the singing? Only for those who join in the
singing is there vocal music: the listener confronts it as absolute music.

Opera, however, begins, according to the most explicit
testimonies, with *the listener's demand to understand the
words.*

What? The listener *makes demands?* The words are to be
understood?

———

To place music in the service of a series of images and
concepts, to use it as a means to an end, for their intensification and clarification—this strange presumption, which is

found in the concept of "opera," reminds me of the ridicu-
lous person who tries to raise himself into the air by his own
bootstraps: what this fool and opera in accordance with this
concept are trying to do are pure impossibilities. This concept of the opera demands of music not so much an abuse
as—to say it again—an impossibility! Music never *can* become a means, however one may push, thumbscrew, or tor-
ture it: as sound, as a drum roll, in its crudest and simplest
stages it still overcomes poetry and reduces it to its reflection. Opera as a genre in accordance with this concept is
thus less a perversion of music than it is an erroneous representation in aesthetics.

When, incidentally, I justify the nature of opera in this
way for aesthetics, I am naturally far from any wish to justify bad opera music or bad opera texts. The worst music, as
opposed to the best poetry, can still signify the basic Dionysian world ground; and the worst poetry, as opposed to the
best music, can still be a mirror, an image, a reflection of
this basic ground. For the single sound, as opposed to the
image, is already Dionysian, and the single image, together
with concept and words, is already Apollinian, as opposed to
the music. Even bad music together with bad poetry can
teach us something about the nature of music and poetry.

Schopenhauer, for example, experienced Bellini's *Norma*
as the fulfillment of tragedy, regarding both the music and
the poetry. In his Dionysian-Apollinian excitement and
self-oblivion, he was totally entitled to feel that way, for he
experienced music and poetry in their most general, quasi-
philosophical value, as music and poetry as such, although
his judgment proved that his taste was not well educated,
that is, not schooled in comparative history.

In this inquiry we deliberately avoid all questions concerning the historical value of an artistic manifestation and try
to focus solely on the manifestation itself in its unchanged
and quasi-eternal significance and thus also in its *highest
type*. Hence the genre of opera seems as justified to us as
does the folksong, insofar as we find both the fusion of the

Dionysian and the Apollinian and presuppose that opera—
meaning the highest type of opera—and the folksong had
an analogous origin. Only insofar as opera, as known to us
through history, has had since its beginnings an origin altogether different from that of the folksong, we repudiate this
kind of opera, for its relation to the generic concept of opera
that we have just now defended is like that of a marionette
to a living human being. Although music certainly can never
become a means in the service of the text and in any case
triumphs over the text, it assuredly becomes bad music
when the composer breaks the Dionysian power that wells
up in him by anxiously observing the words and gestures
of his marionettes. If the librettist has offered him no more
than the usual schematized figures with their Egyptian regularity, then the value of the opera will be greater in direct
proportion to the freedom with which the music unfolds in
its unconditional, Dionysian way, and to the contempt it
shows for all so-called dramatic demands. Opera in this
sense, of course, is at best good music and only music,
while the imposture that goes on at the same time is, so to
say, merely a fantastic disguise of the orchestra, and, above
all, of its most important instruments, the singers, something on which people of insight turn their backs, laughing.
If the crowd finds precisely *this* delightful while taking the
music *in the bargain*, then it behaves like those who esteem
the golden frame of a good painting more than the painting
itself. Such naive aberrations scarcely require a serious or
indignant refutation.

What is the significance of opera as "dramatic music"
when it is as far removed as possible from pure, self-
sufficient, entirely Dionysian music? Imagine a variegated,
passionate drama that carries the spectators along, assured
of success as an action. What could "dramatic" music add,
even if it did not take away anything? In the first place, it
actually will take away a great deal, for at every point where
the Dionysian power of the music strikes the listener like
lightning, the eyes that behold the action and were absorbed

in the individuals appearing before us become moist, and the listener *forgets* the drama and wakes up again for it only after the Dionysian spell is broken. But insofar as the music leads the listener to forget the drama it is not yet "dramatic" music. But what kind of music is it that *may* not exert any Dionysian power over the listener? And how is it possible? It is possible as *purely conventional symbolism* from which convention has sucked all natural force—a music that has been weakened to the point where it is no more than mnemonic devices—and the aim of its effect is to remind the spectator of something that he must not miss while watching the drama if he wants to understand it, as a trumpet signal is for a horse a command to trot. Finally, before the drama begins, and in minor scenes or in dull places whose relation to the dramatic effect is dubious, and even at the highest moments another kind of music that is no longer purely conventional mnemonic music is permitted: *music that aims at excitement* as a stimulant for jaded or exhausted nerves. In so-called dramatic music I can distinguish only these two elements: conventional rhetoric and mnemonic music on the one hand and a music that aims at excitement by means of primarily physical effects on the other. Thus it alternates between noisy drums and bugles, like the mood of a soldier going into battle. Yet a mind schooled in comparisons and finding delight in pure music requires a *masquerade* to conceal these two abuses of music: "reminders" and "excitement" are to be sounded, but in the form of good music that must be enjoyable and even valuable. What a desperate situation for the dramatic composer who has to mask his big drum with good music that nevertheless must not have a purely musical effect but is to produce nothing but excitement! And now a large Philistine public approaches, nodding with a thousand heads, and enjoys this "dramatic music" that is always ashamed of itself, lock, stock, and barrel, without so much as noticing any shame and embarrassment. Rather it feels how agreeably its fur is being tickled, for it is receiving homage in all sorts of ways—though it is a sybarite craving diversions, faint-eyed, in need of excitement, well-bred and thinking much too well of itself, as used to good drama and good music as to good food without ever making much of any of this, a forgetful and absent-minded egoist who has to be led back to the work of art by means of force and bugles because selfish plans concerning profit or enjoyment keep going through his mind all the time. Wretched, dramatic composers!

> Look at your patrons from close up!
> One half is cold, one half is crude. . . .
> With such an aim, you wretched fools,
> Why do you plague the lovely muses?

And that the muses are being plagued, and even tortured and tormented by them, they themselves do not deny, if they are as honest as they are unfortunate!

We presupposed a passionate drama that carried the listener along and was assured of its effect even without music. But I fear that what is "poetry" in it and not just "action" is likely to be related to true poetry much as dramatic music is to music as such: it will be a poetry of reminders and excitement. The poetry will serve as a means to remind people in a conventional way of feelings and passions whose expression was discovered and made famous, even normal, by real poets. Moreover, one will rely on it to help out the real "action," whether that is a horror story of crime or something magical, crammed with mad transformations, and to spread a gentle veil around the crudeness of the action itself. Overcome by shame that the poem is only a masquerade that cannot stand the light of day, such "dramatic" poetizing demands "dramatic" music. On the other hand the poetaster who writes dramas of this sort is met more than half-way by the dramatic composer with his talent for drums and bugles and his fear of genuine music that is self-confident and self-sufficient. And now they see each other and embrace, these Apollinian and Dionysian caricatures, this *par nobile fratrum!*

INDEX

121

Designer: Laurie Anderson
Compositor: Interactive Composition Corporation
Text: 10/13 Trump Medieval
Display: 18/19 Jenson Roman
Printer: Maple-Vail Book Mfg. Group
Binder: Maple-Vail Book Mfg. Group